Savoring the Spice Coast of India

Fresh Flavors from Kerala

Maya Kaimal

Photographs by Ruven Afanador, Zubin Shroff, and John Bentham

Designed by Ph.D

HarperCollins_Publishers_

SAVORING THE SPICE COAST OF INDIA. Copyright © 2000 by Maya Kaimal. All rights reserved. Printed in the United States of America. No part of this book may be used or reproduced in any manner whatsoever without written permission except in the case of brief quotations embodied in critical articles and reviews. For information address HarperCollins Publishers Inc., 10 East 53rd Street, New York, NY 10022.

HarperCollins books may be purchased for educational, business, or sales promotional use. For information please write: Special Markets Department, HarperCollins Publishers Inc., 10 East 53rd Street, New York, NY 10022.

FIRST EDITION

Designed by Ph.D

Photographs by Ruven Afanador on front cover and pages ii, vi, 8, 9, 12, 32, 116, 125, 126-7, 160, 201, 209, 221.

Photographs by Zubin Shroff on pages 5 (top), 16 (top), 20, 25, 36, 53, 64, 68, 80, 84, 92-93, 109, 121, 136, 145, 149, 157, 169, 184, 193, 196, 213, 216.

Photographs by John Bentham on pages 16 (bottom), 45, 61, 89, 100, 113, 123, 130, 173, 176, 181, 183, 224.

Printed on acid-free paper

Library of Congress Cataloging-in-Publication Data

Kaimal, Maya.

    Savoring the spice coast of India: fresh flavors from Kerala/Maya Kaimal.

       p. cm.

Includes index.

    ISBN 0-06-019257-7

    1. Cookery, India. 2. Cookery—India—Kerala. I. Title.

    TX724.5.I4 K23 2000

    641.5954′83—dc21   99-086758

00 01 02 03 04 ❖/   10 9 8 7 6 5 4 3 2 1

Frontispiece: A temple elephant gets a bath at the Guruvayur Sri Krishna Temple near Thrissur.

To Mum and Aunty, inspiring women and wonderful cooks

Contents

Colored powders for Hindu temple ceremonies.

Acknowledgments

First I wish to thank my father's sister, Kamala Nair. My love of family and my love of food are what led me to write this book, and it was in the warmth of my aunty's kitchen in Kottayam, in Kerala, that I saw, again, how food and family fit together. Thank you for being such an inspiration.

Many family members in Kerala shared their recipes, their time, their homes, and their love: Padma, Mini, Nisha, Suchu, Ambika, Sreelatha, and Meenakshi. Other families generously took me into their kitchens, opening my eyes to the incredible variety of Kerala's culinary tradition. Warm thanks go to Nimmy Paul of Kochi, C. P. Moosa and Faiza of Kozhikode, the Ashrafs of Thrikkakara, Haseena Sadick of Kochi, and Mrs. B. F. Varughese of Kottayam.

I am greatly indebted to George Dominic, Executive Director of the Casino Group of Hotels, for his support and guidance, which proved invaluable in my research. Sincere thanks, as well, to those in Kerala who kindly selflessly offered their time and knowledge: Chef Jose Varkey of the Casino Hotel; Palampadom Avarachan; Manarcad Mathew; Dr. V. Venu; Varghese Thomas of Four Foods; Alin M. Hassaier of Frys; A. P. M. Gopala Krishnan of Bestotel; P. S. Abdulla Koya; G. Premnath; and V. C. Nawaz. My research was also generously aided by T. Balakrishnan at the Government of India Tourist Office, and the Kerala Tourism Development Corporation.

I am grateful, as always, to my agent, Jane Dystel. And to Susan Friedland, my editor, for making it possible to write about the food I love the most. Vanessa Stich and Ellen Morrissey both worked hard and carefully on this book and helped make the experience a pleasure. Thank you to the photographers whose work brings Kerala to life on these pages: Ruven Afanador, Zubin Shroff, and John Bentham. And thanks to Michael Hodgson at Ph.D, whose design provides an elegant framework for the recipes.

So many people helped shape this book through their support and advice:

Major N. P. Raja; Vimala Raja; Evelyn Letfuss; David Finkelstein; Margo True; Susan Westmoreland; Dana Cowin; Jane Sigal; Jill Armus; Daneet Steffens; Rebecca Okrent; Mr. Ali of Malabar Palace; and Ron Morrison at Eastman Kodak Company. I also owe special thanks to Padma Kaimal and Andrew Rotter, Narayan Kaimal and Elissa Grad, for all their affection and encouragement. To Guy Lawson, who has shown such faith in me and seen me through difficult moments, thank you for helping me find my way.

My parents, Chandran and Lorraine Kaimal, have given me the confidence and desire to write cookbooks. Cooking with them is a true pleasure because lovely things always happen in, and come from, their kitchen. Thank you both.

Introduction

I was nine when I first went to Kerala, the boyhood home of my father where the lush tip of India meets the Arabian Sea. I'd heard stories about this place, seen photographs, and even tasted the lively South Indian curries my father cooked in our suburban Boston home. Still nothing prepared me for how extraordinarily exotic it would seem when I stepped off that Indian Airlines plane, inhaling the humid musky air, and seeing nothing but coconut palms for miles.

Kerala is a narrow state along the southwestern coast of the Indian peninsula. It's a strikingly beautiful area, densely covered in tropical vegetation, rich in spices, and laced with rivers, lakes, and lagoons—a marked contrast from the great dry plains of Northern India. My father spent his childhood in a small town in the center of the state called North Parur, but left India in 1954 as a young man, to pursue a graduate degree in the United States.

The author's grandparents, Ambuja and K. Narayana Kaimal, holding Aunty Kamala (left) and the author's father, Chandran (right), in 1933.

He had only returned twice in twenty years, and now, in 1974, he was back with his American wife and their three children.

As we crossed the hot tarmac of the modest-looking Kochi (formerly Cochin) airport, I saw a sea of eager faces waiting to greet passengers. The men were in white shirts and *mundus* (a sort of full-length sarong), the women wore patterned silk saris, and little girls in dresses had dark *khol* drawn around their eyes. As we approached, a few of the faces smiled warmly, and I suddenly recognized my father's sister Kamala, her husband, Uncle Chinnappan, and my cousins Padma and Mini from the posed black-and-white studio portraits we'd receive in the mail. Our eyes turned moist as we wordlessly grasped each other's hands, and although I found it odd that we didn't hug like Americans, I felt an instant connection to these people and this place that would deepen over the years and change my life and career.

We squeezed into two hulking white Ambassador sedans and drove to Aunty Kamala's house in Kottayam, a city about 30 miles south of Kochi. The car, a carbon copy of all the other models on the road, had hard bench seats and seemingly nonexistent shock absorbers. My uncle maneuvered the rutted roads, narrowly avoiding oncoming trucks, oblivious cows, and clusters of pedestrians, as only a seasoned Indian driver can do. My wide eyes took in rows of one-room shops overflowing with red bananas and bumpy gourds, stacks of bright fabrics, and gleaming bronze cooking vessels. There was color everywhere, especially on the women, who wore brilliantly colored silk saris edged in gold, with their hair in long black braids that flicked as they walked. All these shades seemed especially bright against a vibrant green backdrop of rice paddies and broad-leafed banana trees. This place is beautiful, I thought, my bare legs sticking to the vinyl car seat, and very very hot.

After winding through a maze of streets and lanes we arrived at the house my grandfather built, a two-story whitewashed home with a red tile roof, set in a compound filled with palm trees and potted bougainvillea. Having just spent the two prior weeks hustling through the ancient monuments of Northern India, the five of us felt relieved to be in Aunty Kamala's quiet, comfortable home. My father changed out of his trousers into a long cotton *mundu*, and we all sat drinking sweet tea as the conversation alternated between English and Malayalam, the melodic, vowel-rich language that rolls off the tongue of everyone from Kerala.

It took me a little while to adjust to spicy food three times a day, but since my aunt is such a skillful cook, I couldn't resist tasting everything that came out of her kitchen. The family is Hindu, and while most Hindus in Kerala eat fish, abundant in the lakes and streams, the cooking tends toward vegetarian fare. From the fruits and vegetables in her garden, my aunt conjured up "dry" curries, "wet" curries, curries with coconut, curries with yogurt, hot chutneys, sour pickles, and highly seasoned *dhals* (legumes).

For breakfast Aunty served slightly sour steamed rice dumplings called *idli*. I liked eating mine with sugar but they are meant to be served with a chutney made from freshly scraped coconut, ginger, and chilies, and seasoned with mustard seeds and a fresh herb called curry leaves (not related to the dry spice mixture called curry powder). Brown mustard seeds and curry leaves, I soon discovered, were in nearly everything. When heated in oil, the seeds release a mellow nutty flavor and the leaves lend a bright citrusy aroma which, together, permeate the cooking of Kerala.

At midday we ate the main meal of the day. My aunt would serve a large pile of rice topped with seasoned dhal, and such curries as fish poached in coconut milk, okra in a yogurt sauce with crushed mustard seeds, pumpkin simmered with toasted coconut, a hot pickle or two, and crisp legume wafers called *pappadam*. Everything was served together on a wide stainless steel plate, with the rice and dhal covering most of it, and small portions of the other colorful foods around the rice.

As with all the food in Kerala, this meal was eaten with the fingers of the right hand (the left hand is considered impure and never touches food). The technique is second nature to South Indians: they combine the rice, dhal, and a crunched-up *pappadam* with a bit of curry, and in a gesture that's a cross between tossing and cupping, they form that mixture into a ball and pop it in their mouths. In an example of the cultural rivalry that exists between the North and South, North Indians never let the food go above the first knuckle when they eat, and they consider Southerners terribly crude since they let food touch their whole hand. In turn, South Indians think Northerners are hopelessly finicky for only using their fingertips. When I tried to eat, I was much less adept than my cousins, and I usually ended up dropping half the food before getting it to my mouth. It's considered poor manners in India to let rice or any food drop, especially off the plate, but I comforted myself with the story that, as a boy, my father used to be so mortified when pieces of rice fell off his plate, that he hid the grains in his shirt pocket.

Every afternoon around five, as the sun lowered behind the coconut trees, I became accustomed to hearing the sound of cups clinking in the kitchen, as Aunty prepared the afternoon tea, making a large pot from dark, South Indian leaves and lots of milk. For a tea snack she would dip bananas in egg batter and fry them in flavorful coconut oil, or deep-fry crisp fritters made of yellow legumes and asafetida. This is the time of day when Indians pay social calls, so there was always enough food for friends or relatives who might stop by. According to Indian hospitality, it would be rude not to offer a visitor food, and even more rude for that visitor not to accept it. Aunty's teatime meals were substantial enough to hold us until dinner, a light affair eaten around 9 P.M. For dinner, at the end of a daily routine defined by the rhythms of mealtimes, she would make a vegetable stew simmered with cinnamon, cloves, and coconut milk. We'd blissfully soak up this stew with her *dosas*, the sourdough rice and legume crepes as delicate as doilies, that are a unique and emblematic feature of South Indian cooking.

Twenty years later, my passport is filled with visas marking my many returns to India. On these visits I've traveled from North to South India, and over time I've come to understand that my aunty's *dosas* are part of the larger story of South Indian cooking. History is written in books, but for the Malayalees (the people of Kerala) it also exists in recipes and ingredients and the language of the kitchen. The Hindu tradition, combined with waves of outsiders who arrived on the shores of Kerala, created the region's unique cooking. Vegetables stir-fried with mustard seeds and fragrant curry leaves, fish cooked with a dried sour fruit preservative called *kodumpuli*, shellfish in silky coconut milk sauces, meat curries with crushed peppercorns, and pancakes made from fermented rice batters capture the past and present of the spice coast.

The North of India, a world away from the climate and cultures of the subtropical South, has a notably different history and, with it, notably different tastes in food. The heartier, milder fare that is typical of the North was, to a great extent, introduced by Mughal invaders from Central Asia who ruled over much of India from the sixteenth to the eighteenth centuries, but whose control never reached as far south as Kerala. With the Mughals came Persian pilaf, which became Indian pulao, the use of dried fruits and nuts, marinated meats barbecued in tandoori ovens, and a fondness for rich lamb dishes.

The great plains of North India are ideal for growing wheat and herding cattle, so Mughal cooking evolved into a cuisine in which wheat flat breads were used to scoop up thick meat and vegetable curries, and such milk products as ghee (clarified butter), yogurt, and cream enriched and thickened the sauces. The arid climate made it necessary to dehydrate vegetables and dry spices for use throughout the winter. In order to add depth to the curries, North Indians toast whole spices before grinding them into *masalas*. This is the cooking that Americans think of as "Indian food," perhaps because it is immensely popular in India and thus became the standard cooking of Indian restaurants here. But in truth, the subcontinent boasts countless regional cooking styles, from the slightly sweet cooking of Gujarat, where jaggery (unrefined sugar) is generously used, to the cuisine of West Bengal where fish and mustard oil are mainstays, to the vibrant green chili and coconut curries of the South.

Aunty Kamala (center) with members of her family. The family home in Kottayam, 1953.

The flavors of South India had a powerful pull on me, and with every visit I felt myself falling more deeply under their spell. Futhermore, my curiosity about the cooking has given me a special connection to my relatives there. I was raised in a family that relished good food and both my parents have exceptional skills in the kitchen. Since we spent a lot of time talking about food at home in New England, it felt completely natural to do the same in my aunt's house in Kottayam. Aunty Kamala always made me feel comfortable in her airy kitchen, as she shared her culinary wisdom and told me stories of growing up with my father.

When my aunt and father were young, the state of Kerala did not exist, but was three distinct regions: Travancore to the south, Cochin in the center, and Malabar to the north. Travancore and Cochin were ruled by maharajas who had considerable autonomy, and Malabar had been part of Madras Province and under British rule since 1799. The people of the three regions spoke Malayalam, so when India's state lines were drawn according to language groups nine years after Indian Independence (1947), all three were combined to form present-day Kerala.

After spending some years in Malaya (now Malaysia), my father's family moved back to Kerala, this time settling in the Travancore town of Kottayam, when my grandfather was appointed to establish and direct the Rubber Research Institute. The southern part of Kerala has a thriving rubber industry, and orderly groves of rubber trees are visible everywhere. On my first trip we visited the institute and its grounds, and I marveled at how workers attached half coconut shells to grooves cut into the tree trunks, and how the sap collected in the shells was transformed into sheets of rubber.

Kerala's nutrient-rich soil and two annual monsoons make it a fertile agricultural area. Today, its primary crops include rubber, rice, coconut (and its by-products), cashews, coffee, tea, and such spices as black pepper, ginger, cardamom, and cinnamon. In order to irrigate the fields and transport the harvest, a network of canals was carved into the Kerala countryside connecting the lakes and inlets. For centuries, graceful long wooden cargo boats laden with goods have floated along these waters, pushed by men with long poles to the ports where the cargoes would be processed or traded.

The spice coast, a fertile stretch of shoreline running along the southern and western reaches of the Indian peninsula, has drawn traders since antiquity. The vast array of peoples that came in search of its natural abundance of black pepper and other spices have given the region a tolerance and openness toward outsiders that continues to be at the core of this unusually harmonious society. Arabs were among the first outsiders to navigate their way to the coast in the tenth century B.C., and for centuries they alone controlled access to the trading ports there. Many Arab traders made this region their home, and by marrying Hindu women they merged the two cultures into what would become the Mappila (Kerala Muslim) community of Kerala. Ancient Greeks and Romans coveted black pepper for medicinal and culinary purposes, and discovered how to use the monsoon winds to speed them across the Arabian Sea to the ancient northern port of Muziris (Kodungaloor today). In return, they brought fennel and fenugreek from the Mediterranean. The Chinese also established trade contact there, introducing the wok, which is still used (in a modified version) as the Indian *kadhai*, and bringing the huge ceramic pots that Indians used for preserving pickles.

Trade with Europe exploded after the Portuguese explorer Vasco da Gama circumnavigated the African Cape of Good Hope and became the first European to chart a sea route to the spice coast, or what is historically known as the Malabar Coast. His fleet landed at the northern port of Kozhikode (Calicut) in 1498, sparking a contentious era of trade between Europe and the spice-rich coast of India. After roughly 200 years of dominating the lucrative spice trade, the Portuguese lost control to the Dutch, who in turn were outmaneuvered by the British in the seventeenth century.

Although this period was marked by conflicts and repression, the Europeans did make notable contributions to the Malabar Coast: the Portuguese encouraged the commercial cultivation of coconut; the Dutch did the same with rice; and the British established tea plantations that gave rise to a profitable export industry. The Portuguese also imported New World ingredients to Kerala, such as the cashew, pineapple, and papaya, but it was the chili pepper they brought that was destined to become one of the most important elements in all of Indian cooking.

Despite Kerala's accessibility by water, there was surprisingly little exchange with its inland neighbors. This was largely due to the long mountain range called the Western Ghats that stretches along the western portion of Southern India, dividing present-day Kerala from Karnataka in the north, and Tamil Nadu in the south. The lush foothills of this range, called the Cardamom Hills, are cooler than the lowlands, and ideal for growing tea, coffee, pepper, and cardamom. The higher rockier peaks, measuring as much as 9,000 feet, were formidable enough to keep out the forces that affected the rest of the subcontinent, including the Mughal Empire.

In antiquity, long before traders and others arrived on the spice coast, there were many influences that reached the ancient agrarian people of this land. These included Jainism, Buddhism, Sanskrit, and early forms of Hinduism, the caste system, and *Ayurveda* (the Hindu science of medicine). Hinduism became the dominant religion there, and a large portion of the Hindu population was (and is) a group called *Nayars*, to which my father's family belongs. This group is roughly equivalent to the *Kshatriya*, or warrior caste. The Nayars, in the old Kerala worldview—before modern time blurred social roles—were positioned below the *Nabuthiris* (priests) and above the *Ezhavas* (formerly toddy tappers), *Mukkavans* (fishermen), and *Kammalans* (artisans).

A number of distinctly Nayar traditions have become synonymous with Keralan culture, including an unusual matrilineal system of inheritance, in which property is passed through the female line. Unlike the rest of India, where a wife joins her in-laws' home, a Nayar woman traditionally lived in *her* family's home. This system was legally phased out in the 1950s, but I can feel its legacy in my own family because my cousins Padma and Mini have homes on the family property that belonged to my aunt, and our maternal grandparents before her.

Wedding garlands hang at a Trivandrum flower market.
Elephants decked out for a Pooram festival in Thrissur.

Other features of the Nayar community include a gymnastic form of martial arts called *Kalaripayattu* and a theatrical dance known as *Kathakali* in which stories from Hindu mythology are enacted by men with bright costumes and dramatic makeup who master precise control over every muscle in their body and face. My family was lucky enough to attend an authentic *Kathakali* performance in 1974 that started at midnight. Despite my childish sleepiness, I was taken by how the vivid expressions, precise gestures, and thrum of the tabla brought the stories to life.

Since Nayar households often contain joint families, there are plenty of hands to help with the vegetable chopping and masala mixing that produce the day's curries. The old stucco and wood homes called *tharawads* were a series of adjoining rooms framed in teak, organized around a central courtyard where the women of the household would boil, dry, and pound the harvested rice to remove the husks. Almost no one processes rice at home anymore, but this grain is still at the center of life in these and all South Indian households.

Rice, legumes, and vegetables dominate the Nayar diet. The sourdough crepes (*dosa*) and dumplings (*idli*) made from rice and legume batters provide a daily staple for most Nayars. This community is widely praised for its vegetable curries seasoned with mustard seeds and fresh curry leaves, and its numerous legume (*dhal*) preparations—the main source of protein in their largely vegetarian diet. Nayars also enjoy eating fish, and their favorite dishes use such sour elements as tamarind and unripe mango. Coconut milk, meat, and oil all add an incomparable flavor and richness to their cooking.

The best way to experience Nayar cooking is at one of their lavish feasts, usually reserved for weddings and *Onam*, the harvest festival, and *Vishu*, the new year's celebration. For these events, more than a dozen classic Nayar vegetarian curries are served with rice, three legume dishes, *pappadam* (wafers), pickles, and puddings. All the dishes are artfully arranged on a large clean banana leaf, looking like a delectable painter's palette.

Approximately 60 percent of Kerala's population is Hindu, the majority Nayar, while the rest is divided between Christians and Muslims, plus very small numbers of Jews, Jains, Sikhs, and Buddhists, each of these groups having a long history in the region. Three of Kerala's communities—the Syrian Christians, the Mappilas (Kerala Muslims), and the Cochin Jews—have developed distinctive cuisines that synthesize their traditions and religious strictures with locally abundant ingredients, among them rice, coconut, green chilies, fresh curry leaves, and tamarind.

In writing this book, I returned again to India to find out more about the traditions and cooking of the Christian and Mappila and Jewish peoples of Kerala. I read their histories and met with many women who generously let me into their kitchens and taught me the recipes and subtleties of their unique cuisines. This experience opened up a huge part of Kerala that I never truly grasped on earlier visits.

The next largest presence in Kerala after the Hindus is the Christian population, a group that dates its origins in the area to A.D. 52 when St. Thomas the Apostle is believed to have visited the Malabar Coast and founded several churches. Although there is some debate surrounding this legend, it is undisputed that a large influx of Christians came to the area from Baghdad, Nineveh, and Jerusalem in the year 345, and it is this group to which the Syrian Christians trace their lineage. Ancient records tell of land set aside for Christian churches by local rulers, and of how this highly motivated group secured prominent positions for themselves in merchant guilds and other aspects of commerce. Their large white churches, designed in a Portuguese style, are a striking presence throughout the landscape, primarily in southern and central Kerala.

The Syrian Christians have continued to distinguish themselves in Kerala society by establishing colleges, creating a huge publishing industry, and being active and successful entrepreneurs. Names like George, Thomas, and Jacob grace many of the businesses in the cities, and their involvement in education, combined with a traditional emphasis on learning fostered by local Hindu rulers, helped catapult Kerala's literacy rate to over 90 percent. Christian women are well educated and encouraged to be professionally ambitious, and the fact that the most prominent cookbook authors and food columnists in Kerala are from this community is no accident. They are intensely proud of their cooking tradition, and they have the determination to turn it into their careers.

Their cuisine reflects the climate, their religion, and their connection (through the church) with Europeans, especially the British. One of their trademarks is the *appam*, or pancake, which is generally made from a slightly sweet, yeasty batter that ferments easily in the hot climate. These pancakes, sometimes lacy, sometimes thick, are designed to be eaten with "stew," a beef or chicken dish in a coconut milk sauce. Since Christians have no religious restrictions concerning meat, they enjoy it all, and are

A blend of Indian and British styles at the Lake Palace Hotel in Thekkady.

regarded as experts at preparing beef, pork, chicken, and such wild game as duck and boar.

A number of English cooking terms have been absorbed into the Syrian Christian lexicon, including stew, roast, and fry. The poultry "roasts" are made with either whole eggs or large pieces of a bird and are cooked with a small amount of sauce in a covered pan. The meat comes out succulent, if a little messy to eat with your hand. Beef and goat are often tough in India, so the Syrian Christian cooks showed me the technique they devised for "meat fry" in which they boil pieces of meat with spices then stir-fry them in a little oil and liquid until very tender.

A favorite way of the Syrian Christians to eat pork is *vindaloo*, a curry made with vinegar and loads of chili powder, introduced by the Portuguese. The Syrian Christian fish dishes I tasted, on the other hand, are pure Kerala, using methods like wrapping whole fish in a banana leaf and steaming it, or stewing it in a deep red sauce flavored with the sour *kodumpuli* fruit. Vegetables are prepared simply, steamed in a little turmeric and red chili powder, then sautéed with mustard seeds.

The European influence is most evident in the desserts. Syrian Christian cookbooks I looked at read like English cookbooks, full of fruitcakes, shortbreads, and puddings. Ovens are not a traditional fixture in an Indian kitchen, and became part of home cooking only after Europeans settled here. Today, though, many affluent Christians own ovens, and use them for baking sweets, especially at Christmastime when they exchange cake with friends and colleagues.

Muslims make up approximately one fifth of the population of Kerala — concentrated in the North, the area still referred to as Malabar. This group, called Mappilas, is thought to be descended from Arab traders who married local Hindu women ("mappila" means bridegroom). A long tradition of trade between the Malabar Coast and West Asia brought (and still brings) a constant flow of Arabs to these shores. When Islam arrived in Kerala, probably in the ninth century, it was able to spread due to the presence of pre-Islamic Arab traders who were friendly to the faith. Once the Mughal powers took hold over the northern part of India, a kind of distant kinship was established between the Muslims in North India and Kerala, which in turn influenced the cuisine.

The Mappilas have played an important role in Kerala's history. During the period when the Portuguese controlled the flow of spices, Mappilas were recruited by the *Zamorins* (Hindu rulers of Malabar) to form a powerful navy to resist the Portuguese fleets. They traditionally worked in trade and agriculture, but the oppression they experienced under a feudal system sparked periodic revolts, and ultimately mobilized them into labor unions. An unusual feature of Kerala politics is the strong Marxist element, as seen in the sickles and hammers painted on walls and buildings across the state. I had always noticed these symbols and the striking laborers marching through town, but only now do I understand the connection between the labor unrest in Malabar and the left-leaning politics of Kerala.

When traveling there, I was struck by how different Malabar looked from the southern part of Kerala I'd always visited. Everywhere minarets of mosques poke up past the coconut trees, and the two-story houses are painted shades of blue and green, unlike the pure white homes with low sloping roofs in the South. The men wear small fitted caps to cover their heads, and all the women wear head scarves and learn the labor-intensive art of Mappila cooking from the age of ten.

The cuisine of the Mappila community blends local fish, coconut, bananas, curry leaves, and tamarind, into North Indian Mughal meat curries and rice casseroles (*biriyanis*). A delicious chicken *kurma* I tried in Malabar is a perfect example of how these elements marry. This North Indian classic was thickened with a paste made from fresh coconut and raw cashews, replacing the traditional cream used in the north. Mappila *biriyanis* are equally fascinating amalgams, featuring goat, fish or shrimp, coconut, and curry leaves. These extraordinary casseroles (and most Mappila curries) are finished with a North Indian–style garnish of sautéed nuts and raisins.

Other traces of Mughal cooking that appear here are the liberal use of garam masala (the North Indian spice blend with cinnamon, cloves, cardamom, and nutmeg), ghee, fresh coriander, and mint. This cuisine includes no pork, since it is forbidden in Muslim culture, but it is otherwise known for its rich meat preparations made with quantities of onions sautéed slowly until sweet, plus a wide array of ground spices including fennel and star anise, resulting in deep, layered flavors. To accompany the meat and chicken curries, Mappilas make a number of breads, from simple rice-flour flat breads to decoratively folded deep-fried yeast breads, all of which taste wonderful wrapped around a bit of meat curry. Plain rice is rarely eaten by this community, which prefers the North Indian style of eating curries with bread.

There is a complexity to this cuisine, both in technique and flavor, that sets it apart from the Hindu and Christian food in Kerala. Members of this community told me that the cooking became so refined because Mappila women are raised with the expectation that they will spend their days in the kitchen, preparing delicacies for their husbands. And, in fact, they do produce some remarkable dishes, particularly for wedding feasts and during Ramadan and the festival of Id when they turn out platters of meat pastries, stuffed breads, banana fritters, and egg puddings. This amazing cooking opened my eyes to just how diverse the cuisines within the small state of Kerala actually are.

The last group that fascinated me, the Cochin Jews, turned out to be the most elusive, since most have left Kerala for Israel and other parts of the world. The Jewish presence in Kerala plausibly dates back to the fifth century, while trade contact between Israel and the Malabar Coast goes back as far as 1000 B.C. when King Solomon reigned. Copper plates from the time recorded that the Jews were welcomed by the local rulers, and, in the ancient tradition of toleration of others, allowed to practice their faith freely. Their most famous and recent enclave was in Fort Cochin, the busy trading port of central Kerala. The Rajah of Cochin granted them land for their synagogue—a pleasant airy building that still stands—in an area that became the center of the spice trade and matter-of-factly named "Jew Town."

This community of prosperous merchants, traders, and spice processors, retained their own customs, but spoke Malayalam and dressed in the loose cotton clothing of the locals. Much of the indigenous vegetarian fare suited them, since it fit their kosher laws, but their cuisine (which also included fish and poultry) was continually influenced by the tastes of the most recent wave of Jews to arrive there. Iraqi Jews were the last group to settle in Cochin, so their taste for fresh coriander, garlic, cumin, and hot chilies has largely prevailed. The ubiquitous coconut, of course, worked its way into their cuisine, as did locally grown tamarind, and curry leaves, resulting in such lively dishes as fish poached in a coconut and fresh coriander sauce, and chicken stewed with green chilies and tamarind.

It was a delicious journey to discover, firsthand, many of the rich traditions within Kerala. And it was especially satisfying to learn that each community delights in each other's specialties: all Malayalees look forward to eating Hindu vegetarian dishes during the annual harvest festival, Christians give Christmas cakes to their non-Christian friends, and everyone covets an invitation to a Muslim wedding to eat *biriyani*. There is a Malayalam word for this phenomenon: *pakarcha* meaning sharing, or more specifically, the exchange of food between those celebrating a holiday and their friends and neighbors of different religions.

I felt honored to have been invited into so many households and shown recipes passed down through generations, allowing me to take my passion for Kerala further than I'd ever imagined. My aunty's cooking was an inspiring introduction for me, and now I'm pleased to be able to bring this exceptional cuisine to others. This is food that cannot be ordered in restaurants and, in a sense, I hope it never is. After all, the best Indian food is always eaten at home.

Advice to Get Started

A typical meal in Kerala includes four or five different curries, but feel free to make just one dish and have it with non-Indian food. The idea is to bring new flavors and seasonings to any table and any meal.

This book offers a sampling of the region's delicacies. Given the subtle variations from one city to the next, and one family to the next, it would be impossible to record every dish from the region. I chose to include a wide range of classic recipes that represent different traditions, religious communities, and tastes, vegetarian and nonvegetarian.

This section provides some tips to help make sense of this cuisine in your kitchen with ingredients that are easily available. Try starting with a simple menu and allow yourself plenty of time. This food is not complicated, but it requires a little organization and the patience to chop and measure the ingredients.

Ingredients

Most of the ingredients are readily available in good quality supermarkets, health food stores, and Indian groceries. One exception is *kodumpuli*, a real signature of central Kerala's fish curries that is quite difficult to get here, so I've substituted tamarind, a similar-tasting fruit sometimes used interchangeably with *kodumpuli* in India. In place of some of Kerala's gourds and vegetables, I've called for roughly equivalent, easy-to-find replacements, for example: cucumber for ash gourd, zucchini for snake gourd, and butternut squash for Indian pumpkin. One ingredient worth seeking out is the fresh curry leaf (see page 26), since it adds a layer of flavor that cannot be approached with any other ingredient. The curries will still be good if you don't use it, but it's part of what makes Kerala's food so delicious.

Indian cooking is about taking the time to prepare the ingredients well, not complicated techniques, so take the time to cut and measure everything before starting to cook. Assemble all your ingredients in bowls, ready to go, for each recipe, and the cooking will proceed smoothly. A friend says she likes making this food because she feels like an alchemist in the kitchen, mixing spice blends and grinding pastes.

However, all that alchemy will surely go to waste if you undersalt this food. It cannot be stressed enough how crucial salt is in allowing the flavors of the seasonings to come forward. Without salt, a recipe will taste flat. I always do a final taste of a dish before I serve it, something my aunt does routinely, and very often it needs a few more grains of salt to give a full flavor. One of our family's principles is that there should be a comfortable balance of salty, hot, and sour flavors. If a dish tastes as if it is missing something, try adjusting those elements, using additional salt, chopped green chili or cayenne, and lemon juice.

Techniques

A technique to master is seasoning the oil, a process referred to as *tarka* in some parts of India. It's simple to do: heat vegetable oil slightly; add mustard seeds and *cover the pan*; when most of the seeds have popped and turned grayish, add a dried red chili and brown it slightly; add curry leaves and stand back as they sputter. This can be the first step (in a stir-fry), or the last step (in a wet curry or cooked dhal).

A process repeated throughout this book is preparing a masala paste with coconut and ground spices. In South India this would be done on a flat grinding stone with a pestle the size of a rolling pin. The aim is to produce a thick, finely pulverized paste with a minimum amount of water. Lacking a grinding stone, blenders are the next best tool because they achieve a finer texture than food processors.

There is another method for beginning a curry intrinsic to Indian cooking, and it is as follows: brown the aromatics (onion, ginger, garlic) in oil; add the ground spice masala and fry until the spices lose their raw smell; add tomato (or other liquid ingredient) and fry until a paste is formed and the oil can be seen separating from the mixture; then add the main ingredient, i.e., vegetable, fish, poultry, or meat. This process gives the spices time to mellow—something which is essential for a well-balanced, deeply flavored curry. Because of this, Indian vegetables taste best well cooked, not *al dente*. The most important thing is to pay attention to how things look, smell, and sound as you are cooking this food, so check the pan frequently for subtle changes.

If you do choose to make a number of dishes, stagger the cooking so you aren't trying to finish five curries at the same time. Each recipe indicates what can be done ahead of time; as a general rule, chicken and meat dishes can be finished hours or even a day ahead (and acquire a deeper flavor that way), but fish should always be made just prior to serving.

Equipment

This list of essential tools will help you prepare this food with ease:

> A variety of nonstick pans including: a chef's pan (a deep frying pan),
> > a 12-inch frying pan, a 10-inch griddle
>
> A Dutch oven or heavy casserole dish with a lid
>
> A large wok with a lid
>
> A mortar and pestle (or coffee grinder used only for spices)
>
> A blender
>
> A food processor (or mini food processor)
>
> A full set of measuring cups and spoons

These tools are useful for making the more specialized items. They are sold in Indian grocery stores:

> An *idli* steamer
>
> A *sev* (noodle) press
>
> An *appam* pan

The Kerala Pantry

This glossary of South Indian ingredients lists everything by their English and Malayalam names. Before you start cooking from this book, visit an Indian grocery store or health food store and stock your pantry with some basics: ground spices, brown mustard seeds, dried red chilies, a few dhals, coconut, coconut milk, and tamarind. It will cost less than twenty dollars, the ingredients will keep for up to a year, and you won't have to hunt for ingredients when you want to cook this food. If you don't live near a store that carries these items, you can order most of them from the mail-order sources listed at the end of this chapter. Fresh curry leaves will require a trip to an Indian or Asian store (or you can purchase the plant, see page 31), but fresh green chilies and cilantro are probably carried by your local supermarket. Once your pantry is outfitted, you'll soon discover it's simple and inexpensive to make this complex-tasting cuisine.

Fresh curry leaves, dried red chilies, and mustard seeds: cornerstones of Kerala's cooking.

ASAFETIDA (*KAYAM*)   The dried ground form of this powerful-smelling resin is used in combination with fenugreek seeds to flavor dhals and pickles in South India. It has a strong, sulfurlike odor, but when a pinch is fried in oil its fragrance is like truffles. It should be used sparingly or it will overpower a dish. Store in an airtight container.

ATTA FLOUR OR *CHAPPATHI* FLOUR   Indian whole wheat flour, called *atta*, is made from low-gluten wheat milled to a fine powder. It makes a beautifully soft dough, perfect for flat breads such as *chappathis* and *parathas*. If it is not available, substitute half all-purpose and half standard whole wheat flours.

BASMATI RICE   See Rice.

BITTER GOURD (*PAVAKKA*)   Also called bitter melon, this vegetable has a thick, spiny light green skin and large seeds. The less ripe the gourd, the more tender and edible the seeds, but once the seeds become tough they should be removed before cooking. The skin, however, is always left on. Indians sometimes blanch it first to mellow the bitterness, and it's tastiest when fried to a deep golden brown. When selecting a bitter gourd, look for one that is firm without yellow spots or wrinkled areas.

BLACK PEPPER (*KURUMULAKU*)   The combination of Kerala's climate and soil yields some of the largest, most flavorful peppercorns in the world. Before Portuguese traders introduced chili peppers from the New World, black pepper was the primary hot ingredient in Indian food. But black pepper with its sharp bite continues to be a flavor component, particularly in South Indian cooking. Whether the peppercorns are crushed, coarsely ground, or powdered greatly changes the effect they have on the curry, so take note of the form used in each recipe.

BUTTERMILK (*MORU*)   Unlike the thickened version sold in the United States, Indian buttermilk is the leftover liquid from freshly churned butter, and has a thinner texture and less sour flavor. Both Syrian Christians and Hindus in Kerala have thin tangy buttermilk curries that they serve over rice with fish curry. Commercial buttermilk is a satisfactory substitute.

CARDAMOM (*ELAKKA*)   This spice is native to the hills of eastern Kerala. The small pods are harvested, dried, and sometimes bleached, but unbleached green cardamom has the most delicate flavor. This versatile spice has a sweetly aromatic flavor that enhances meat curries, rice dishes, and desserts. Buy whole pods—not ground cardamom—and split them open by applying pressure with the side of a knife or a pestle. Use the tip of a knife to scoop out the small seeds, discard the husk, crush and then grind the seeds with a mortar and pestle or in a grinder used only for spices.

CASHEW NUTS (*KASHUNANDI*)   Cashews arrived in India from Brazil by way of the Portuguese. The plants thrived in Kerala's climate, and today South India is one of the world's leading exporters of cashews. Only raw, unsalted nuts are used in cooking; they are either fried in ghee (clarified butter) for a garnish, or ground into a paste to thicken a curry. It's not necessary to buy whole nuts because the broken pieces work fine in these recipes.

CAYENNE OR GROUND RED PEPPER (*CHUVANNA MULAKU*)   This is the dried powdered form of ripe capsicums otherwise known as red chili peppers. In Kerala they use Kashmiri chili powder, which has a bright red color and a tempered heat. Since that type is milder than the cayenne we purchase here, South Indian curries can take on a pretty shade of red without being overwhelmingly hot. Use our cayenne judiciously, because if overdone, its heat is sharp on the back of the throat.

CHANNA DHAL   See Dhal.

CHILIES, DRIED RED (*ONAKIA MULAKU*)   Whole dried red chilies are one of the many forms of the capsicum to lend heat to South Indian curries. Browned in hot oil together with mustard seeds and curry leaves, dried chilies help form the trademark seasoning of a Kerala curry. Some cooks break the chilies open before adding them to the oil, thereby releasing the seeds and making the dish hotter, but I prefer to leave them whole. They are sold under different names, but look for chilies that are 2 to 3 inches long, deep red, and unbroken.

CHILIES, FRESH GREEN (*PACHA MULAKU*)   Fresh chilies have a more fruity, vegetablelike flavor than red chilies. Since they grow year-round in Kerala, chilies are used in their fresh green form to add zing to almost every savory dish. The pungent element called capsaicin is contained in the oil within the seeds, so deseeding is one way of eliminating their intensity. The method used by most cooks is to slit the chili from the bottom tip to about 1/4 inch from the stem, leaving the seeds only partially exposed.

This gives cooks more control over the heat of a dish than if they chop the chili: if, partway through the cooking, the curry tastes too spicy the slit chili can be removed. I suggest using serrano or Thai chilies, but jalapeños could be used in a pinch. If your hands are very sensitive to the capsaicin, you may wish to use disposable gloves when handling them.

CILANTRO (*KOTHAMALLI*)　The fresh leaves of the coriander plant have a lively herbal flavor—quite different from the earthy, lemony taste of ground coriander seeds from the same plant—that makes curries sparkle. The flavor fades with cooking, so add it just after removing a curry from the heat. Always buy it fresh, not dried, and use the leaves and tender stems for cooking. In Kerala it is primarily used in Muslim cooking.

CINNAMON (*KARUVAPATTA*)　Another spice from Kerala, cinnamon adds a sweet and intense perfume to chicken and meat curries. Often used in combination with whole cloves, cinnamon stick brings a rich aroma to Kerala's outstanding coconut milk stews. It is also one of the ingredients in garam masala, the sweet and hot spice blend found in Muslim dishes across India, such as *kurma* and *biriyani*.

CLOVES (*GRAMBU*)　Cloves originated in the Spice Islands (Indonesia), and were probably brought to India for cultivation by Portuguese spice traders. Whole cloves are the dried unopened flower buds of the clove tree. Their sweet yet sharp flavor adds a warm layer to the same meat and vegetable curries in which cinnamon is used. In its ground form it is one of the ingredients in the spice blend garam masala.

COCONUT (*THENGA*)　The coconut tree is perhaps the single most important commodity in Kerala. It supplies wood for scaffolding, palm fronds for thatched roofs, fiber for rope, and of course, many forms of food from the fruit. The form most often used in cooking is freshly grated or scraped coconut. After the nut has been cracked in two with a heavy blade, the inside of each half is rubbed against a serrated blade, shredding the meat into a snowy white pile. The grated meat is ground with spices on a grinding stone to produce thick masala pastes for flavoring curries. Fresh coconut has an exceptionally good flavor; however, lacking the proper tools, I make do with dried unsweetened grated coconut sold in Indian markets or health food stores, and grind it in a blender with spices and a little water to make a masala paste. Buy finely grated coconut, or process the coarse type in a blender—otherwise it is too fibrous for these

curries. For desserts I find sweetened shredded coconut works perfectly well. But some dishes in Kerala use coconut slices (small chips made from fresh coconut) for which there is no convenient substitute. So if you want to achieve authenticity, the method for preparing them is provided on page 220. Dried or fresh coconut should be wrapped well and stored in the freezer.

COCONUT MILK (*THENGA PAL*) North Indians use cream to thicken their curries, but South Indians use coconut milk. This "milk" is the juice pressed out of grated coconut mixed with hot water. The process is always done twice: the "first milk" is richer and will curdle if boiled, so it's added at the end of cooking; the "second milk" is more watery and can be cooked for a long time without breaking down. I find using canned coconut milk infinitely easier than extracting fresh milk, but I still follow the principle of using thinned coconut milk initially, then adding undiluted canned coconut milk at the end. Coconut milk spoils quickly, so if you don't plan to use it within a day, freeze the unused portion.

COCONUT OIL   See Oils.

CORIANDER (*KOTHAMALLI*)   Ground coriander seed is the dominant spice in South Indian cooking. It has a lemony flavor, and it's used as a thickener in chicken, egg, and meat curries. I recommend purchasing ground coriander (not seeds, which can be difficult to grind finely) and storing it in an airtight container away from the light.

CREAM OF RICE (*IDLI RAVA*)   A coarsely ground rice product called *idli rava* in India offers a short-cut to grinding rice from scratch. The breakfast cereal called Cream of Rice is essentially the same, so it makes a perfect substitute.

CUMIN (*JEERAKAM*)   Cumin is like the bass note of Indian cooking: it provides an indispensable layer of flavor, especially in vegetable curries. Preground cumin is used most often in Kerala, but occasionally the seeds, resembling caraway seeds, are dropped into hot oil to flavor it for a stir-fry. It's useful to have both whole seeds and ground cumin on hand. The ground cumin sold through Indian grocery stores and mail-order sources has a high turnover and so tends to be fresher than what is sold in supermarkets. But if you prefer to grind your own cumin with a mortar and pestle, be sure to use only two thirds of the amount called for in the recipe because the taste will be stronger.

CURRY LEAVES (*KARIVEPILA*)   This fragrant herb is a signature flavor in the cooking of Kerala. It has no relationship to the mixture of ground spices called curry powder, except that both come from the Anglicized version of the Tamil word *kari*, or sauce. The taste falls somewhere between green bell peppers and citrus peel, but like cilantro, the flavor is fleeting. Ways to capture its essence include sizzling the leaves in hot oil (the *tarka* method) and adding them at the last stage of cooking. There are roughly twenty flat leaves attached to each stem, and the leaves are stripped off the stem much like thyme. Fresh curry leaves, sold at Indian and Asian markets, are the most flavorful form by far, and I have discovered how to keep them fresh and green for up to 6 weeks: Remove them from their plastic bag; pat them dry of any moisture; place them in between dry paper towels; store them in a large airtight Ziploc bag in the refrigerator. Some people keep them in the freezer for months, which is slightly better than using the dried leaves that have little taste. Another option is growing a curry leaf plant (*murraya koenigii*), not to be confused with the small, silvery "curry plant," named for its curry powder scent. It's a temperamental bush, but I know people who have been successful at growing it and cooking with it (see mail-order sources, page 31).

CURRY POWDER   The term evokes the image of a strong-smelling yellow powder promising to transform anything into an instant "curry." But this spice blend has little to do with the way people traditionally make curries in India. In order for each dish to be finely nuanced, a home cook must grind and mix the spices fresh for each recipe. To make the recipes in this book, it is a simple matter of combining ground spices for each dish; none of them use commercial curry powder.

DHAL (*PARIPPU*)   The word broadly encompasses the many dried legumes (split and whole) used in Indian cooking. Dhal can be cooked with seasonings to make a dish by the same name, or soaked and ground into batters for pancakes, dumplings, and fritters; sometimes a small handful is fried in hot oil—like a spice—to add crunchiness to a vegetable or rice dish. The dhals used in these recipes should be purchased skinned and split (except skinned whole mung dhal), and if purchased from an Indian or Asian store they should be washed first in plenty of water to remove dust and debris. Channa dhal, or Bengal gram, is a light yellow, rounded legume similar to yellow split peas. Masoor dhal is small, flat, and coral-colored although it turns yellow when cooked. Mung dhal, or green gram, looks like very small, pale yellow spheres when the green skin is removed. It is a whole legume and has an especially nice flavor when roasted. Thoor dhal, also called red gram, is fairly flat and golden and has a pleasant earthy flavor; do not buy the oiled variety. Urad dhal, or black gram, is small, oval, and creamy white-colored (the husk is black), and it is either ground into batters, or fried in oil to add texture to a curry.

FENNEL SEED (*PERUMJEERAKAM*)   The Malayalam name for this spice means "big cumin" since it resembles a cumin seed but is plumper and greener. Its delicate licorice flavor enhances chicken and meat curries in Kerala. Always crush the whole seeds for the best flavor.

FENUGREEK (*ULUVA*)   These small, square, golden seeds add a bitter-butterscotch flavor to South Indian fish curries, *sambar* (a spicy lentil stew), and pickles. The seeds are usually used whole since they are hard to crush, but if the recipe calls for powdered fenugreek, I suggest using a mini food processor or a clean coffee grinder. Use sparingly—too much of this spice makes a curry taste bitter.

GARAM MASALA   The name of this ground spice mixture means "hot spices" in Hindi and it is an important ingredient in North Indian cooking. Although the elements vary according to individual tastes, this homemade blend usually includes sweet and hot spices such as: cinnamon, clove, cardamom, and black pepper. In Kerala, the Mappilas (Muslims) use a version that also includes nutmeg, star anise, and fennel in their *biriyanis* and meat curries. See the recipe on page 222.

GARLIC (*VELUTHULLI*)   Fresh garlic is used in most Indian cooking except by certain Hindu sects, who shun it as an aphrodisiac. It is part of the aromatic mixture (along with onion and ginger) that is at the base of a large number of curries, especially fish, poultry, and meat.

GHEE (*NEYYU*)   For a cuisine that predates refrigeration by thousands of years, it was essential for Indian cooks to find ways of extending the life of perishable foods like butter. Ghee, the solution, is a nutty-tasting form of clarified butter that has been slowly simmered until all the moisture evaporates and the milk solids precipitate to the bottom and brown slightly. With all water removed, it will keep, covered, at room temperature for up to a month, or refrigerated for 6 months. Ghee has a higher smoking point than butter, and Kerala Muslims prefer it over vegetable oil as a cooking medium. Hindus like to pour a spoonful over their rice and dhal. See the recipe on page 218.

GINGELLY OIL See Oils.

GINGER (*INJI*)   A plant native to Kerala, this sharp-tasting rhizome is one of the cornerstones of the region's cuisine. Fresh-sliced ginger adds a peppery quality to coconut milk stews, and chopped ginger is an essential aromatic in fish, poultry, and meat curries, and chutneys.

KODUMPULI   This very tart fruit also goes by the name "gamboge" and is used in Southern and Central Asian cooking. In Kerala, where it is very popular with Hindu and Syrian Christian cooks, it is sometimes called "fish tamarind" because it is used to remove fishy odors and flavor fish curries, plus it has a taste similar to regular tamarind. The fruit is sold in dried rubbery-looking segments, and although it appears almost black, it releases an orange pigment when soaked in liquid. It has a very high acid content, so in addition to lending a sourness, it acts as a preservative in fish curries, making it possible for them to keep for days without refrigeration. It is possible but difficult to find this ingredient in the United States, so I call for regular tamarind in its place for the recipes in this book.

MASALA   This term is used in Indian cooking to refer to a spice mixture (wet or dry) used to flavor a dish.

MASOOR DHAL AND MUNG DHAL   See Dhal.

MUSTARD SEEDS (KADUGU)   An essential ingredient in South Indian cooking, tiny brown mustard seeds have a pungent flavor when raw, but turn pleasantly nutty when fried in oil. One of the distinctive features of Kerala cooking is to "pop" mustard seeds in oil, then add a dried red chili and curry leaves, all of which aromatize the oil of the curry—a process known as *tarka* in some parts of India. When heated, mustard seeds release their moisture and actually make a popping sound as they jump in the pan. For this reason, it is best to place a cover over them during this process. Although milder tasting yellow mustard seeds are not used in India, they may be used in place of brown.

OILS (ENNA)   Any mild-tasting vegetable oil such as canola, sunflower, safflower, corn, or even peanut oil, works well for most of these recipes. Olive oil is not suitable because its flavor is too strong and distinctive for this type of cooking. The preferred cooking oil in Kerala is, of course, coconut oil, which despite being highly saturated, is also highly delicious. There are a few recipes that rely on its rich smoky flavor, so I do recommend using small quantities of it in a few recipes. However, if you have health concerns it can be omitted. Coconut oil has a low smoking point which makes it less versatile than other oils. The oil also spoils more quickly than most oils and should be refrigerated. It turns into a white solid when cold, so place the bottle in warm water to melt it when you need to cook with it. Gingelly oil is a golden-colored Indian sesame oil with an unassertive flavor. In Kerala it is used for frying crepes (*dosa*) and pancakes (*uthappam*), and for making pickles. It can be replaced with regular vegetable oil mixed with a few drops of dark Chinese sesame oil.

ONIONS (ULLI)   Frying sliced onions in oil is the first step of many Indian curries. They give body to the sauce, providing flavor and thickness. A type of small purple onion, similar to our shallot, is used in most cooking in Kerala. I generally use yellow onions sliced very thin for this type of cooking; large white onions are too coarse and don't break down as easily when cooked. Shallots have a milder flavor and more delicate texture than yellow onions, and for some recipes I find them preferable but not essential.

POPPY SEEDS, WHITE (*KHUSKHUS*)   Muslim cooking in North and South India uses ground white poppy seeds as a thickener in meat curries. I do not recommend substituting black ones because they turn the sauce a grayish color, so simply omit poppy seeds from the recipe if white ones are not available.

RED CHILI   See Cayenne.

RICE (*ARI*)   In Kerala, "parboiled" rice is eaten with curries. Sometimes sold as rosematta, parboiled rice is a harder, more nutritious grain that is cooked in boiling water like pasta. If you can find parboiled rosematta rice, by all means use it, but if not, serve plain long-grain or basmati rice with curries. Basmati rice, the aromatic grain of Northern India, is predominantly eaten by Muslims in Kerala and is ideal for their rice casseroles known as *biriyanis*. Although it is not traditional in the South, plain basmati can also be served with curries, but should not be used for making South Indian pancakes, crepes, or dumplings. Use only regular long-grain rice for those dishes.

RICE FLOUR (*ARI PODI*)   This flour is used for making noodles, pancakes, and breads, and is always freshly milled on an as-needed basis in Kerala. The fine, powdery rice flour sold here works perfectly well in making these dishes. I give instructions to lightly roast the rice flour first—also done in Kerala—to remove any excess moisture.

SALT (*UPPU*)   An essential ingredient, salt helps bring forward the complex flavors of Indian cooking. Remember that Indian curries are always eaten in combination with rice or bread, which balances a strongly flavored dish. These recipes were formulated using crystallized salt, so if using kosher salt you will need to increase the amounts.

STAR ANISE (*THAKKOLAM*)   The sweet strong licorice flavor of this spice is part of the Mappila (Kerala Muslim) spice blend, *garam masala*. It complements meat curries and adds an extra perfume to *biriyanis*. In its whole form it has a tough woody texture, so a coffee grinder or mini food processor is useful for grinding it.

TAMARIND (*PULI*)   South Indians have a penchant for sour things, especially the tart, fruity pulp of the tamarind pod. Sold in a fibrous pressed block or as a thick smooth concentrate, tamarind is always dissolved in water, and the tangy juice (no solids) is added to vegetable, fish, and chicken curries.

THOOR DHAL See Dhal.

TURMERIC (*MANJAL*) The bright yellow color associated with commercial curry powder comes from the powder of this dried rhizome. Its brilliant color makes it an excellent fabric dye, as well as adding a golden tint to food. Turmeric's flavor, however, is bitter and woody and should be used sparingly and in combination with other ground spices.

URAD DHAL See Dhal.

YOGURT (*THAYIR*) Most Indians make "curds" (yogurt) at home. In the South it is served with a final portion of rice at the end of a rice meal as a palate cleanser. Sometimes it is used in cooking as a sour element. Use plain low-fat or nonfat yogurt for these recipes, or put out a bowl of it with rice and curries.

Mail-Order Sources for Ingredients

Adriana's Caravan
BROOKLYN, NEW YORK
800-316-0820 (TEL)
212-972-8849 (FAX)
www.adrianascaravan.com

Kalustyan, Orient Export Trading
Corporation
NEW YORK, NEW YORK
212-685-3451 (TEL)
212-683-8458 (FAX)
www.kalustyans.com

Penzeys Spices
MUSKEGO, WISCONSIN
800-741-7787 (TEL)
414-679-7878 (FAX)
www.penzeys.com

Source for curry leaf plants:
Bhatia Nurseries
DIVISION OF P. C. LINK CORPORATION
NEW YORK, NEW YORK
212-221-7040 (TEL)
212-221-7132 (FAX)
www.bhatia-nurseries.com

Creating a South Indian Meal

When planning a meal in Kerala, a cook knows what kind of rice she will serve. If she is Hindu or Christian, she will probably choose plain, boiled rice, or, for a special occasion, perhaps a flavored one such as Lime Rice (page 167). If the cook is Muslim and she wants to make an impressive meal, she will undoubtedly choose to make a *biriyani*, the elegant rice dish baked with spiced meat or fish (pages 170, 172, and 174), or in a simpler mood, she might opt for gently perfumed Ghee Rice (page 168).

The other elements of an Indian meal (curries, pickles, salad) are considered side dishes, since they are served in small portions alongside the rice. This is a particularly Asian approach: serving small amounts of protein (for example, meat, chicken, and fish) with lots of vegetables and rice, and it challenges the Western notion that meat is the main dish and the starch and vegetables are side dishes.

Hindus always serve dhal (seasoned legumes) poured

At a Hindu feast, banana leaves are used as plates for rice, pappadam, *and countless vegetarian dishes.*

over their rice, along with wet and dry vegetable curries, a fish or chicken curry (unless they are vegetarians from the highest priest caste), and pappadam (legume wafers). For the multicourse Hindu feasts that are served on large banana leaves at weddings, Vishu (new year's holiday), or Onam (harvest holiday), the rice, curries, and pickles would be continually replenished; however, the dhal element would be replaced by sambar (legume and vegetable stew, pages 110 and 112), pulisheri (buttermilk curry, page 97), rasam (legume broth, page 114), and yogurt (buttermilk), in sequence. A typical dessert at these feasts would be a sweet milky pudding called payasam (pages 200, 202, and 203).

In a Christian home there would be *thoren* (dry meat curry, page 152), a chicken curry, a fish curry, maybe two simple vegetable dishes, a buttermilk curry (page 97), and pickles. Since their diet includes more meat protein than the Hindu diet, they don't generally serve dhal. At Christmas and Easter, when big feasts are prepared for visiting family members, the meal would become more elaborate by adding a first course featuring a type of *appam* (rice pancake, pages 50 and 52) served with a meat and coconut milk stew (page 154). Dessert on these occasions would be a rich fruitcake (page 206) or custardy pudding.

The Muslims prefer meat, chicken, fish, and seafood dishes to vegetable ones, and they rarely eat dhal. Their meals consist of such rich preparations as stuffed whole fish (page 123), a creamy chicken *kurma* (page 147), and a hearty beef or lamb curry. Yogurt salad, pickles, and chutneys are also part of the Muslim meal. Unlike the Hindus and Christians, the Muslims make fried yeast breads (pages 177 and 178) to accompany curries and *biriyani*. When they prepare grand feasts to celebrate weddings or to break the fast during Ramadan, they prepare *samosas* (page 62) or steamed rice pockets stuffed with meat for a first course, and conclude the meal with *mutta mala*, an elegant egg-based sweet in which the whites are baked into a custard, cut into diamonds, and served over the yolk which has been dripped into boiling sugar syrup until it resembles a stringy garland.

There's no need to follow these traditional menus to enjoy this cooking. When I have a dinner party, I mix and match curries from the Hindu, Christian, and Muslim communities, and they are delicious—albeit not completely authentic—when served together. A meal can be as extravagant as a *biriyani*, with four or five curries, a salad, and a bread, or it can be plain rice and three curries. Another option is to make any single dish from this book and serve it with a non-Indian meal. If you want to incorporate the pancakes or noodle dishes into a menu, try serving them as a first course. Also, the *samosas* (page 62) and fritters (pages 59 and 60) make tasty hors d'oeuvres. And any of the desserts in the Sweets and Beverages chapter are a nice way to round out your South Indian meal.

In India, most meals are eaten without utensils, which can feel awkward to people who were raised believing it's rude to eat with your hands. Not only is it polite to eat with your right hand (the left is considered impure), the food is designed to be eaten this way: the ingredients are cut into bite-size pieces, and the dishes are matched up according to textures that hold together well. In the North, flat bread is used to scoop up bites of thick curries. In the South, though, where rice is the main starch, a good balance of wet and dry dishes is needed to pick up the rice. The important thing is not whether you eat a meal with your hand, but that the meal offers a range of textures and colors and tastes on one plate.

The curries in this book feed approximately six people, if you serve at least four dishes, plus rice. (The same recipes will feed at least eight if you increase the number of curries to five or six.) It is traditional to leave in the whole spices such as green and red chilies, curry leaves, cinnamon sticks, and whole cloves when serving this food. You may remove them before serving; however as long as guests are warned to push them to the side of the plate, it looks much prettier to leave them in.

Here is a basic guide for putting together a South Indian meal for six. Add a first course from among the pancakes and noodle dishes, and a dessert from the sweets chapter, if you wish. For the main course, choose one of the following:

1. A rice (plain, flavored, or *biriyani*)
2. A bread (optional)
3. A dhal
4. A dry vegetable (with or without coconut)
5. A wet vegetable (without coconut if the other vegetable has it)
6. A fish or seafood curry and/or a chicken, egg, or meat curry (or substitute a hearty vegetable curry for a meatless meal)

Tiffin: Appetizers and First Courses

Some of the best food in Kerala is eaten for breakfast or as a snack. Pancakes, dumplings, or noodles provide the starchy element for the lighter meals of the day, whereas rice and curries make up the main meal, eaten at midday. These light meals are sometimes referred to as "tiffin," an Anglo-Indian word meaning "snack," and they usually include one of these starches and a spicy side dish or two. The climate in Kerala is always hot and humid, and certain foods—like the fermented batter for *dosa* (crepes) and *idli* (dumplings)—depend on those conditions, and require extra care to prepare well in cooler places. My father, a retired atmospheric physicist, has been getting tips from our South Indian friends and experimenting with *dosa* batter for years, and if you follow his perfected method described on page 40, you will be successful. It's worth noting that the consistency of the batter is critical, so when stirring in the final addition of water,

Sourdough Crepes (page 40) with Spicy Dhal and Vegetable Stew (page 110) and Red Coconut Chutney (page 189).

err on the side of less because you can always thin it with more water later if necessary.

In Kerala the same batter is used to make lacy sourdough crepes (*dosa*) and fluffy sourdough dumplings (*idli*), and since these are eaten almost daily, there is always a batter at some stage of fermentation in a South Indian kitchen. Both of these are favorite breakfast foods—particularly in Hindu homes—and are eaten with coconut chutney and a spicy dhal stew called *sambar*.

Appam is the Malayalam word for "pancake," and the Syrian Christians in Kerala are famous for making many delicious versions. *Appams* are also fermented, but usually with the help of toddy (fermented coconut sap) or yeast, and they come in different shapes and thicknesses, depending on the pan used. A fragrant coconut milk–based curry called a *stew* is the ideal accompaniment to any of these slightly sweet pancakes at breakfast or dinner.

The snacks served with afternoon tea are usually bite-sized morsels, either savory or sweet, like fritters made from dhal, or pieces of ripe banana dipped in egg batter and fried. Rich and elaborate snacks like *samosas* are the specialty of Kerala's Muslim community, and they are one of the first things eaten when the fast is broken during Ramadan.

Although there isn't always a meal in the West that corresponds with things like the savory breakfast or the teatime snack, you can fit these exceptional dishes into a menu by serving the snacks as hors d'oeuvres and the pancakes, noodles, and dumplings as first courses. Despite the difference in climates, you'll find that the versions in this chapter have been adapted, with much assistance from my physicist-cook father, so that they will work no matter where you live.

Sourdough Crepes (*Dosa*)
Sourdough Crepes with Potato Masala (*Masala Dosa*)
Sourdough Crepes with Vegetables (*Uthappam*)
Sourdough Dumplings (*Idli*)
Savory Breakfast Stir-Fry (*Idli Upuma*)
Savory Breakfast Noodle Stir-Fry (*Vermicelli Upuma*)
Lacy Rice Pancakes (*Palappam*)
Fresh Rice Noodles (*Idiyappam*)
Rice Noodle Stir-Fry
Coconut Rice Pancakes (*Kallappam*)
Sweet Dumplings (*Kozhukutta*)
Dhal Fritters (*Dhal Vada*)
Banana Fritters
Batter-Fried Bananas (*Pazham Pori*)
Spiced Meat Samosas

Sourdough Crepes
(*Dosa*)

¹/₂ cup split urad dhal
1¹/₂ cups long-grain rice (not
　basmati)
¹/₂ teaspoon fenugreek seeds
1 teaspoon salt
¹/₄ teaspoon baking soda
Gingelly oil or vegetable oil for frying

A staple in South India, this lacy pancake is made from a fermented rice and urad dhal batter. The key to proper fermentation is to keep the batter at 90 degrees F. This is effortless in tropical Kerala, but it has taken my father years to perfect in upstate New York. Here is his foolproof method that should work regardless of where you live. Note that you must begin soaking ingredients a full day in advance.

1. Place the urad dhal in a large bowl and rinse with many changes of water until the water no longer appears cloudy. Drain.
2. In a large bowl combine the drained urad dhal with the rice, fenugreek seeds, and 2¹/₂ cups water. Soak the ingredients together for 4 hours at room temperature, until the dhal and rice expand and soften. When a grain of rice just breaks under the pressure of your fingernail, the ingredients have soaked long enough.
3. Drain the urad dhal and rice, reserving the liquid. Place roughly half of the solids and half the liquid in a blender and grind them long enough to get a smooth consistency with some graininess remaining (1¹/₂ to 2 minutes). Test by rubbing a little batter between your fingers. The largest grains should be the size of granulated sugar. Pour the mixture into a large bowl. Repeat the process with the remaining solids and liquid, and add the mixture to the bowl. Stir in the salt. The mixture should be very thick, so it will be necessary to thin it with approximately ¹/₄ cup water to get the consistency of pancake batter.

4. Cover the bowl loosely with plastic wrap and place in an oven, kept warm to a temperature of 90 degrees F for 12 to 15 hours. This can be achieved with the help of a trouble light or floodlight fitted with a 25 watt bulb. Plug the power cord into an outlet close enough to the oven so that the bulb can rest on a rack in the oven. Turn on the light and prop open the door about 1 inch with the handle of a wooden spoon. Check the temperature periodically to be sure it stays at 90 degrees. During warm summer months it may not be necessary to use the lightbulb. The batter should nearly double in volume and smell a little sour.

5. Remove the bowl from the oven and stir the contents. The batter will be thick and foamy. If you choose not to fry the crepes immediately, refrigerate the batter at this point. Remove it from refrigerator half an hour before frying.

6. When ready to fry the crepes, check the consistency of the batter: it should pour smoothly like pancake batter. Add the baking soda, and a little more water if needed.

7. Heat a nonstick griddle or frying pan over medium-low heat (two pans will speed up the process). Spread about $\frac{1}{4}$ teaspoon oil evenly over the griddle. Ladle $\frac{1}{4}$ cup of the batter into the center of the hot griddle, and immediately, using the back of the ladle, gently but steadily spread the batter in a circular motion from the center out, creating a thin pancake. If the batter does not spread easily into a thin layer, thin it with a little more water.

8. As the crepe cooks, small holes will form on the surface. Sprinkle a few drops of oil on top, to help make it crisp. When the bottom turns a golden color (about 1 minute) turn it over and fry the other side 30 seconds or until lightly browned. Fold the crepe in half, golden side out, and place it on a platter. Keep the fried crepes warm as you repeat the process, oiling the griddle each time. Serve immediately.

SOAKING AND FERMENTING TIME: 16 TO 19 HOURS
FRYING TIME: 30 MINUTES
SERVES: 6
YIELD: 18
RECIPE MAY BE PREPARED IN ADVANCE THROUGH STEP 5.

Sourdough Crepes with Potato Masala
(*Masala Dosa*)

Crepes

1 recipe Sourdough Crepes (page 40)

Filling

1 tablespoon channa dhal or yellow
    split peas

3 large boiling potatoes, peeled and
    cut into $1/2$-inch cubes

2 tablespoons vegetable oil

1 teaspoon mustard seeds

$1/2$ teaspoon cumin seeds

8 fresh curry leaves

2 cups sliced onions

1 teaspoon minced ginger

1 teaspoon minced fresh green chili
    (serrano or Thai)

$1/4$ teaspoon turmeric

$1/8$ teaspoon cayenne

$3/4$ teaspoon salt

$1/2$ teaspoon lemon juice

This irresistible South Indian snack of Sourdough Crepes (*dosas*) stuffed with spicy potato curry (masala) is now popular even in North India. Once you've mastered the pancakes, the filling is easy. Note that you need to start the pancakes a day in advance; the filling can be prepared anytime. Serve with any coconut chutney (pages 188, 189, or 190) and *sambar* (pages 110 or 112).

1. Prepare Sourdough Crepes through step 5.

2. Soak the channa dhal in a small bowl of water for 10 minutes. Drain.

3. In a saucepan boil the potatoes in salted water for 8 to 10 minutes, or until they are tender when pierced with a knife. Drain, reserving the liquid for later.

4. In a wide nonstick pan with a lid heat the oil over medium-high heat. Add the mustard seeds and cover. When the mustard seeds have popped, toss in the cumin seeds and curry leaves and shake the pan, allowing the cumin seeds to brown and the leaves to sizzle. Next add the drained channa dhal and fry, stirring constantly until golden. Put in the onions and sauté until soft but not brown, then add the ginger and green chili and fry for 1 minute. Stir in the turmeric, cayenne, and salt and fry for another minute. Finally add the drained potato and $1/2$ cup of the reserved liquid, reducing the heat to medium-low, and simmering, with the cover on. Periodically add more of the potato liquid ($1/4$ cup at a time), and stir occasionally, until the

mixture is pastelike and the potatoes have broken down (about 10 minutes). Stir in the lemon juice and remove from the heat. Cover and set aside.

5. Fry the *dosas* according to the instructions in the Sourdough Crepes recipe. After frying each one, place it golden side down and spoon about 2 tablespoons of the potato filling onto one half. Fold in half, and place the filled *dosa* on a warm platter; cover, while you continue frying the rest. Serve promptly.

SOAKING AND FERMENTING TIME: 16 TO 19 HOURS
FILLING PREPARATION TIME: 1 HOUR
FRYING TIME: 30 MINUTES
SERVES: 6
YIELD: 18
RECIPE MAY BE PREPARED IN ADVANCE THROUGH STEP 4.

Sourdough Crepes with Vegetables
(*Uthappam*)

Pancakes

1 recipe Sourdough Crepes (page 40)

Topping

1/2 cup chopped shallots or red onion

3 fresh green chilies (serrano or Thai), finely chopped

12 to 15 fresh curry leaves, finely chopped (optional)

These thick pancakes are studded with shallots and green chilies, but feel free to substitute different vegetables in the topping, like chopped seeded tomato or peas. Serve with any coconut chutney (pages 188, 189, or 190) and *sambar* (pages 100 or 112).

1. Prepare Sourdough Crepes through step 5.

2. When the batter has fermented and you are ready to fry, check that it is the consistency of cake batter. Add the baking soda and a little more water if needed, and set aside for 10 minutes.

3. Heat a nonstick griddle or frying pan over medium-low heat (two pans will speed the process). Spread about 1/4 teaspoon oil evenly over the griddle. Ladle about 1/3 cup batter onto the griddle, exactly as you would make a pancake. Sprinkle the top surface with a little of the shallots, green chili, and chopped curry leaves. When the underside is well browned, flip over and cook the other side 30 seconds or until nicely browned. Remove to a platter, vegetable side up, cover and keep warm as you fry the rest. Serve promptly.

SOAKING AND FERMENTING TIME: 16 TO 19 HOURS

FRYING TIME: 30 MINUTES

SERVES: 6

YIELD: 12 LARGE PANCAKES

RECIPE MAY BE PREPARED IN ADVANCE THROUGH STEP 1.

Sourdough Dumplings

(*Idlis*)

¹/₂ cup split urad dhal

1¹/₄ cups Cream of Rice (*idli rava*)

³/₄ teaspoon salt

¹/₄ teaspoon baking soda

Idlis are another item that can be made from a fermented rice and urad dhal batter. These lentil-shaped dumplings are cooked in a special three-tiered metal steamer with curved depressions called an *idli* tray, which can be purchased at Indian grocery stores. They are usually served in pairs for breakfast, accompanied by *sambar* (pages 110 or 112) and coconut chutney (pages 188, 189, or 190), but I serve them with these spicy side dishes as a first course for dinner.

1. Place the urad dhal in a bowl and rinse with changes of water until the water is no longer cloudy. Drain.
2. Soak the urad dhal and ³/₄ cup water in a bowl at room temperature for 4 hours.
3. Place the soaked dhal and its liquid in a blender and process on medium speed 2 to 3 minutes or until the batter flows easily inside the blender and the texture feels smooth when rubbed between thumb and forefinger. If the batter does not move easily, add a little more water. Pour the batter into a large bowl.
4. In a separate bowl combine the Cream of Rice and ³/₄ cup water and stir. Set aside for 10 minutes.
5. Add the soaked Cream of Rice to the ground dhal and stir in the salt. The batter should be the texture of thick pancake batter. Cover it loosely with plastic wrap.
6. Place the bowl in an oven, kept warm to a temperature of 90 degrees F for 12 to 15 hours. This can be achieved with the help of a trouble light or floodlight fitted with a 25 watt lightbulb.

Plug the power cord into an outlet close enough to the oven so that the bulb can rest on a rack in the oven. Turn on the light and prop the door open about an inch with the handle of a wooden spoon. Check periodically to be sure the temperature remains constant, and to monitor the batter. During warm summer months it may not be necessary to use the lightbulb. When the batter is fermented it will be foamy, doubled in size, and have a pale golden color. It should also smell a little sour. If you're not planning to steam the pancakes immediately, refrigerate the batter at this point.

7. When you are ready to steam the dumplings, add the baking soda to the batter and set aside for 10 minutes. By now the consistency should be like cake batter. Add a little water if necessary.

8. In a covered pot large enough to hold an *idli* tray (see headnote), place an inch of water. Bring the water to a boil. Spoon enough of the batter into the tray to fill the depressions. The batter should sit thickly in place. Now assemble the tray, place it in the pot, and steam for 10 minutes. Remove the tray and cool for 1 minute. Scoop out the *idlis* with a rubber spatula and place them on a warm platter; cover. Rinse off any bits of *idli* stuck to the trays and repeat with remaining batter.

SOAKING AND FERMENTING TIME: 16 TO 19 HOURS
STEAMING TIME: 30 MINUTES
SERVES: 6 AS A LIGHT MEAL
YIELD: 18
RECIPE MAY BE PREPARED IN ADVANCE THROUGH STEP 6.

Savory Breakfast Stir-Fry
(*Idli Upuma*)

1 recipe Sourdough Dumplings
  (page 46)
3 tablespoons vegetable oil
2 teaspoons mustard seeds
3 dried red chilies
20 fresh curry leaves
1 cup sliced shallots or onion
2 teaspoons finely chopped fresh
  green chili (serrano or Thai)
3/4 teaspoon salt
2 teaspoons fresh lemon juice

In Kerala, leftover *idlis* are turned into a version of the breakfast dish called *upuma*. The recipe below requires one batch of Sourdough Dumplings. Serve with sliced bananas or White Coconut Chutney (page 188) for brunch, or even as a first course for dinner.

1. Prepare Sourdough Dumplings through step 8.
2. Crumble the cooled *idlis* into 1/2-inch pieces or smaller.
3. In a large wok heat the oil over medium-high heat. Add the mustard seeds and cover. When the seeds have popped, add the dried red chilies and curry leaves. After the leaves have crackled for a few seconds, add the shallots and green chili and fry until the shallots are soft. Stir in the crumbled *idlis* and salt and fry over medium heat, stirring constantly for about 5 minutes. Sprinkle a tablespoon or two of water if necessary, to prevent sticking.
4. Add the lemon juice and remove from the heat. Serve warm.

SOAKING AND FERMENTING TIME: 17 TO 20 HOURS
COOKING TIME: 40 MINUTES
SERVES: 6 TO 8
RECIPE MAY BE PREPARED IN ADVANCE THROUGH STEP 2.

Savory Breakfast Noodle Stir-Fry
(*Vermicelli Upuma*)

4 cups broken (1-inch lengths) angel
    hair pasta (about 6 ounces)
1 teaspoon Ghee (page 218) or
    vegetable oil
2 tablespoons vegetable oil
$1/2$ teaspoon mustard seeds
1 dried red chili
12 to 15 fresh curry leaves
$1/2$ cup broken cashews
1 cup finely chopped onion
1 teaspoon minced ginger
1 teaspoon minced fresh green chili
    (serrano or Thai)
$3/4$ teaspoon salt
$1/4$ cup grated unsweetened coconut

PREPARATION TIME: 30 MINUTES
SERVES: 6
RECIPE MAY BE PREPARED AN HOUR
    IN ADVANCE AND KEPT WARM.

For a zesty South Indian brunch, serve this dish with Eggs Stirred with Coconut (page 151), Sourdough Dumplings (page 46), Red Coconut Chutney (page 189), and *sambar* (page 110).

1. In a large wok fry the pasta in the ghee until lightly browned. Remove the pasta to a plate and set aside.

2. In a small saucepan bring $1^1/2$ cups water to a boil. Reduce to a simmer and cover.

3. In the same wok, heat the vegetable oil over medium-high heat. Add the mustard seeds and cover. When the seeds pop, toss in the dried red chili and curry leaves. Fry for a few seconds, then stir in the cashews. When the cashews are golden brown, add the onion, ginger, and green chili and fry until the onion is soft and translucent, but not brown.

4. Add the fried pasta and salt to the fried onion. Stir over medium-high heat and slowly add 1 cup of the boiling water. Continue stirring constantly until the water is completely absorbed (5 to 7 minutes). Gradually add the remaining water in small increments to keep the noodles moist, stirring continuously for another 5 minutes. Test the noodles for doneness, they should be tender but not mushy. You may need to adjust the water and cooking time to get the right consistency.

5. When all the water is absorbed and the noodles are cooked, add the grated coconut and combine. Serve warm.

Lacy Rice Pancakes
(*Palappam*)

¹/₄ cup Cream of Rice (*idli rava*)
¹/₂ teaspoon dry active yeast
7 teaspoons sugar
2 cups rice flour
¹/₄ cup whole milk
¹/₂ teaspoon salt
Gingelly oil or vegetable oil for frying

These delectable rice pancakes, also called "hoppers," are bowl-shaped with thick spongy centers and crisp lacy edges. Although it takes a special steep-sided wok to get the authentic shape, you can come close with a 6-inch nonstick pan. This type of *appam* (pancake) is made with milk and has a sweet yeasty flavor. Syrian Christians like to serve it with Beef in Fragrant Coconut Milk (page 154) as one of the courses of a wedding feast. Serve as a deliciously rich first course.

1. In a small saucepan bring 1 cup water to a boil. Add the Cream of Rice and bring to a boil. Reduce the heat to medium and continue stirring until the mixture becomes very thick (2 to 3 minutes). Remove from the heat and allow to cool.
2. In a small bowl combine the yeast, ³/₄ cup warm water, and 1 teaspoon of the sugar. Set aside for 10 minutes or until foamy.
3. Combine the rice flour and the remaining sugar in a large mixing bowl. Add the cooled Cream of Rice, the yeast mixture, and about ³/₄ to 1 cup water, or enough to make a thick batter; whisk together thoroughly. Cover the bowl loosely with plastic and allow to sit 6 to 8 hours or overnight, at room temperature.
4. After the batter has fermented and doubled in size, mix in the milk and salt. The batter should be like a thin pancake batter; if too thick, thin with more milk. If you are not planning to fry the pancakes immediately, refrigerate the batter at this point. Bring it to room temperature again before frying.
5. Heat an *appam* pan or a 6- to 8-inch nonstick pan over

medium-low to low heat. Add a little oil and smear to coat the surface evenly. Ladle ¹/₄ cup of the batter into the center of the pan. Immediately lift the pan and rotate it to spread the batter into a 6-inch circle. The batter should bubble and form holes. (These pancakes are typically thick in the center and lacy on the edges; however, if made in a frying pan they will be shaped like a pancake.) Cover the pan tightly and cook 4 to 5 minutes until the center is cooked through and the edges and underside are cinnamon brown. *Do not flip over*. Remove with a spatula. Serve immediately, or place on a platter in a warm oven and continue frying the remaining pancakes.

FERMENTING TIME: 6 TO 8 HOURS OR OVERNIGHT
FRYING TIME: 50 MINUTES
YIELD: 12 TO 14
SERVES: 6
RECIPE MAY BE PREPARED IN ADVANCE THROUGH STEP 4.

Fresh Rice Noodles
(*Idiyappam*)

1 cup rice flour
$^1/_2$ teaspoon salt
$^1/_2$ teaspoon vegetable oil
$^1/_4$ cup grated unsweetened coconut

A delicacy in Kerala, these heavenly rice noodles are squeezed through an Indian noodle press into stringy-looking clusters, and steamed until perfectly tender. On my last night at her house, my aunt always makes my favorite meal: *idiyappam* with *sothy* (page 99), a seasoned coconut milk sauce. They also pair nicely with any of the stews or chicken curries that have gravies. Making this recipe requires an Indian *sev* press (available at Indian grocery stores), and a steaming device such as a bamboo steamer or an *idli* tray. The same dough can also be used to make Sweet Dumplings (page 58).

1. In a wok or large frying pan roast the rice flour, stirring occasionally over medium-high heat until the mixture is very hot and wisps of steam are visible rising from the pan. Do not brown. Remove from the heat immediately and set aside. (If the flour is underroasted the *idiyappam* will be tough.)

2. In a saucepan bring 2 cups water, salt, and oil to a boil. Remove from the heat.

3. Place the roasted flour in a bowl. Gradually add $1^1/_2$ of the 2 cups of water, stirring vigorously to moisten the flour and break up the lumps. Continue stirring, or if cool enough, knead by hand in the bowl until the dough is springy, like Play-Doh. If it feels too dry, add more water; if it's too sticky, add a little (unroasted) rice flour. Cover.

4. Take apart an *idli* tray or bamboo steamer. Spread the three trays on a counter and sprinkle them generously with grated

Fresh Rice Noodles with Coconut Milk and Shallot Sauce (page 99).

coconut to prevent sticking. Meanwhile, in a covered pot large enough to hold the steamer bring an inch of water to a boil.

5. Fit the *sev* press with the finest hole attachment ($1/16$-inch diameter). Fill the press with dough and squeeze out nest-shaped clusters of noodles into each depression of the *idli* tray or make four clusters in each bamboo layer. Each one will be 3 inches wide and $1^1/_2$ inches thick in the center. Sprinkle more coconut on top of each mound (this prevents them from sticking together when they are layered on a platter). Assemble the steamer, place it in the pot with the boiling water, cover tightly, and steam for 12 minutes. Remove, allow to cool for a minute, and carefully scoop out each cluster with a rubber spatula, placing them on a platter. Cover.

6. Rinse off any bits of noodle sticking to the steamer, and repeat the process, layering coconut, noodles, and coconut, as before. Check the water level in the pot before steaming. Serve promptly.

PREPARATION TIME: 25 MINUTES
STEAMING TIME: 25 MINUTES
SERVES: 6 TO 8 AS A FIRST COURSE
YIELD: 24
RECIPE MAY BE PREPARED AN HOUR IN ADVANCE THROUGH STEP 3. WRAP THE DOUGH IN PLASTIC
    UNTIL READY TO PRESS IT.

Rice Noodle Stir-Fry

2 tablespoons split urad dhal

¹/₄ cup split channa dhal

2¹/₄ teaspoons salt

¹/₂ teaspoon plus 3 tablespoons
  vegetable oil

8 ounces rice sticks

1 teaspoon mustard seeds

¹/₄ cup broken raw cashew nuts

¹/₄ teaspoon turmeric

1 to 2 teaspoons finely chopped fresh
  green chili (serrano or Thai)

1 teaspoon minced ginger

2 tablespoons fresh lemon juice

SOAKING TIME: 30 MINUTES

PREPARATION TIME: 30 MINUTES

SERVES: 4 TO 6

RECIPE MAY BE PREPARED AN HOUR
  IN ADVANCE AND KEPT WARM.

Here's a lemony noodle dish full of crunchy nuts and dhal that can be made with Chinese rice sticks sold at Asian grocery stores. It's especially popular in Kerala's neighboring state of Tamil Nadu, where it would be eaten as a snack. I double the recipe and bring it to potluck parties.

1. Combine the dhal, rinse, and set aside to soak in water to cover for 30 minutes. Drain.

2. In a large pot bring 3 quarts water to a boil. Add 1 teaspoon of the salt and ¹/₂ teaspoon of the oil. Toss in the rice sticks and boil 2 to 3 minutes or until *al dente*. Remove the pot from the heat and allow to sit for 2 minutes. Drain thoroughly and set aside.

3. In a wide nonstick frying pan, heat the remaining 3 tablespoons oil over medium-high heat. Add the mustard seeds and cover. When the seeds finish popping, put in the cashews and the dhal, and stir until the nuts turn golden brown.

4. Add the turmeric, green chili, ginger, and the remaining 1¹/₄ teaspoons salt; stir for another 30 seconds. Mix in the drained rice sticks and stir-fry, chopping the noodles into roughly 2- to 3-inch pieces. Fry until the rice sticks lose their excess moisture and the flavors blend (about 5 minutes). Taste for salt.

5. Remove the mixture from the heat and stir in the lemon juice. Serve warm or at room temperature.

Coconut Rice Pancakes
(*Kallappam*)

1 teaspoon active dry yeast

2 cups rice flour

$^1/_4$ cup Cream of Rice

1 cup grated unsweetened coconut

4 teaspoons sugar

$^1/_2$ teaspoon salt

1 cup canned coconut milk

$^1/_2$ teaspoon vegetable oil (optional)

These thick pancakes are a specialty of the Syrian Christian community in Kerala. My friend Nimmy Paul explained to me that they used to be fermented with toddy (liquor made from the sap of a coconut tree), but because reliable toddy is hard to come by these days, most people use yeast instead. Serve them as a first course with Nimmy Paul's wonderful Coriander Chicken (page 146), or with Eggs with Spicy Masala (page 150), or Shrimp in Coconut Milk (page 133). Note that the batter must be prepared at least 6 hours before frying.

1. Combine the yeast and $^1/_2$ cup warm water in a small bowl and set aside for 5 to 10 minutes, until frothy.

2. In a wok or wide skillet heat the rice flour over medium heat, stirring constantly, until the flour is warmed through and wisps of steam are visible rising from the pan. Do not brown. Set aside to cool.

3. In a small saucepan combine the Cream of Rice with 1 cup water. Bring the mixture to a boil, reduce the heat to low, and stir constantly for 2 to 3 minutes or until it becomes moderately thick. Remove from the heat; cool.

4. In a large bowl whisk together the proofed yeast, the rice flour, cooked Cream of Rice, coconut, sugar, and about 1 cup water, or enough to make a very thick batter. Set aside in a warm, moist place (such as in an oven with a bowl of hot water) for 6 to 8 hours or until the mixture expands slightly and appears bubbly. At this point, the batter can be kept refrigerated

for hours. Bring to room temperature before frying.

5. Just before frying, add the salt and coconut milk to the batter and stir. Add a little more water, if necessary, to get the consistency of frothy cake batter.

6. Heat a nonstick griddle or nonstick frying pan over medium heat (or if using cast iron, add $1/2$ teaspoon of vegetable oil). Ladle $1/4$ cup of batter onto the center of the hot griddle as you would pancake batter. It should sit thickly on the griddle, and many small bubbles will form. When the underside has dark brown spots the color of cinnamon, flip it over and brown other side. The pancake should be about $1/2$ inch thick and laced with fine holes. Remove to a platter and cover to keep warm. Continue to fry the remaining batter.

FERMENTING TIME: 6 TO 8 HOURS
FRYING TIME: 40 MINUTES
YIELD: 18 TO 20
SERVES: 6 TO 8
RECIPE MAY BE PREPARED IN ADVANCE THROUGH STEP 4.

Sweet Dumplings
(*Kozhukutta*)

1 recipe Fresh Rice Noodles (page 52)
½ cup grated sweetened coconut
¼ cup packed brown sugar
¼ teaspoon cumin seeds, ground finely with a mortar and pestle or coffee grinder
¼ cup grated unsweetened coconut

I think of these as Indian dessert dim sum because the outside has the texture of a Chinese steamed dumpling. *Kozhukutta* are made from the same dough as Fresh Rice Noodles, but are formed into smooth balls with meltingly sweet centers. If you're preparing Fresh Rice Noodles, you can use part of the dough to make a few of these as a sweet snack.

1. Prepare Fresh Rice Noodles through step 3. Keep the dough wrapped in plastic.
2. In a small saucepan, combine the sweetened coconut, brown sugar, and ground cumin seeds over medium heat. Stir until the mixture becomes a dark sticky paste, but not so dry that the coconut gets brittle. Remove from the heat.
3. Break off enough dough to make a 1-inch ball. Press the ball with your hands to form a thin disk. Place a teaspoon of coconut filling in the center of the disk and roll between your palms to form a smooth, seamless ball. If there are any cracks the filling will leak out when steamed.
4. Sprinkle some unsweetened coconut on each layer of an *idli* tray or bamboo steamer to prevent sticking. Place eight balls on each layer so they aren't touching each other.
5. In a covered pot large enough to hold the steamer bring an inch of water to a boil. Place the assembled steamer in the pot, cover tightly, and steam for 18 minutes. The dumplings are cooked when their texture is springy. If they are pasty, cook them longer. Serve warm or at room temperature.

PREPARATION TIME: 30 MINUTES
COOKING TIME: 18 TO 20 MINUTES
SERVES: 6 TO 8
YIELD: 24
RECIPE MAY BE PREPARED IN ADVANCE THROUGH STEP 3.

Dhal Fritters
(*Dhal Vada*)

¹/₂ cup split urad dhal
¹/₂ cup thoor dhal or yellow split peas
³/₄ cup finely chopped onion
2 teaspoons minced ginger
1¹/₂ teaspoons minced fresh green
   chili (serrano or Thai)
¹/₄ cup chopped cilantro
Ground masala
   • ³/₄ teaspoon cumin
   • ¹/₄ teaspoon cayenne
   • ¹/₈ teaspoon asafetida
1¹/₂ teaspoons salt
Vegetable oil for deep-frying

SOAKING TIME: 4 HOURS
PREPARATION TIME: 20 MINUTES
FRYING TIME: 30 MINUTES
YIELD: 25 TO 30
SERVES: 8 TO 10
RECIPE MAY BE PREPARED IN
   ADVANCE THROUGH STEP 3 AND
   KEPT AT ROOM TEMPERATURE.

These savory snacks are often served at teatime in South India. My aunty always serves this variety with small, sweet bananas, but I also like them with Green Coconut Chutney (page 190) as an hors d'oeuvre.

1. Combine the dhal in a medium bowl, and rinse in several changes of water until the water no longer appears cloudy. Cover the dhal with 1 inch of water and soak at least 4 hours at room temperature.
2. Drain the dhal thoroughly. Place it in a food processor with 2 tablespoons water and process to the texture of couscous, or until a clump of the mixture holds together when pressed into a ball. Scrape the mixture into a medium mixing bowl.
3. Add the onion, ginger, green chili, cilantro, ground masala, and salt to the dhal. Combine thoroughly.
4. In a wok, heat the oil to 325 to 350 degrees F. Wet the palm of one hand slightly, and into that cupped hand place a spoonful of batter to form a 1¹/₂ x ¹/₂-inch lentil-shaped disk; place on a large plate. Continue forming disks, spreading a little water on the palm of your hand each time. Fry 5 to 6 *vada* at a time. Cook to a deep golden brown, turning occasionally for about 5 minutes; drain on paper towels. Serve immediately.

Banana Fritters

4 medium-size ripe bananas, peeled
$^1/_4$ cup whole milk
1 large egg, lightly beaten
1 cup all-purpose flour
1 tablespoon sugar
$^1/_4$ teaspoon baking soda
Vegetable oil for frying

These little pancakes make an excellent snack with tea, or a sweet hors d'oeuvre with drinks.

1. In a bowl mash the bananas with a fork until soft with some chunks remaining. Stir in the milk and beaten egg. Add the flour, sugar, and baking soda, mix thoroughly, and set aside for 10 minutes.

2. In a wide nonstick frying pan heat $^1/_4$ inch of oil over medium-high heat. When the oil is hot, drop spoonfuls of the batter to form 2-inch-wide fritters. Fry them in batches for 2 to 3 minutes on each side until golden brown. Remove and drain them on a paper towel. Serve warm.

PREPARATION TIME: 30 MINUTES
YIELD: 12 TO 16
SERVES: 6 TO 8
RECIPE SHOULD BE PREPARED JUST PRIOR TO SERVING.

Batter-Fried Bananas
(*Pazham Pori*)

1 cup all-purpose flour

1 tablespoon sugar

$1/4$ teaspoon baking soda

Pinch of salt

1 large egg

$1/4$ teaspoon vanilla extract

Vegetable oil for deep-frying

6 firm yellow bananas (no brown spots)

When I smell hot coconut oil around five o'clock in the afternoon, I know my aunt is frying her marvelous batter-dipped bananas to have with tea. Even if you skip the coconut oil as I do, these are a tasty snack; they are also very good with vanilla ice cream for dessert.

1. In a large bowl combine the flour, sugar, baking soda, and salt.

2. In another bowl beat together the egg and vanilla with $1/2$ cup water. Pour this into the dry ingredients and stir until thoroughly combined. It should be a thick batter that coats a spoon.

3. In a large wok heat about 3 inches of oil to 350 degrees F. Line a plate with paper towels.

4. Peel the bananas; slice them in half lengthwise, then cut each one in half crosswise. When the oil is hot, dip the banana slices into the batter and slip them into the hot oil, frying five to six at a time. Fry until they are golden brown (about 3 minutes), turning occasionally.

5. Drain on paper towels and repeat with remaining bananas. Serve promptly.

PREPARATION TIME: 25 MINUTES

SERVES: 6 TO 8

RECIPE SHOULD BE PREPARED JUST PRIOR TO SERVING.

Spiced Meat Samosas

Dough
2 1/2 cups all-purpose flour
3/4 teaspoon salt
5 tablespoons vegetable oil

Filling
3/4 pound beef tenderloin
3/4 cup peeled, cubed boiling
  potatoes
3 tablespoons vegetable oil
1 cup finely chopped onion
1 teaspoon minced garlic
1 teaspoon minced ginger
1 to 2 teaspoons minced fresh green
  chili (serrano or Thai)

Ground masala
- 3 teaspoons coriander
- 1 teaspoon cumin
- 1/4 teaspoon cayenne
- 1/4 teaspoon black pepper
- 1/8 teaspoon turmeric
- 1/16 teaspoon cinnamon
- 1/16 teaspoon clove

1 teaspoon salt
1 teaspoon lime juice
2 tablespoons finely chopped cilantro

Vegetable oil for deep-frying

I visited a Muslim family in northern Kerala who served me tea with half a dozen beautifully prepared Mappila specialties. Everything was delicious, but these dense beef pastries were simply outstanding. The filling has hints of cinnamon and clove that contrast the bright flavors of lime and cilantro. I've found tenderloin gives the best texture. Serve them plain or with Sweet Green Mango Chutney (page 191).

1. Prepare the dough by combining the flour and salt in a bowl, and mixing in the oil. Sprinkle in 1/2 cup water and work in by hand. Add more water if needed to make a stiff but pliable dough. Turn onto a lightly floured surface and knead for 5 minutes, until the dough is smooth. Roll into golf-ball-size balls and set aside to rest for an hour.

2. To make the filling, trim the meat and cut it into roughly 2-inch cubes. Place the cubes in a food processor fitted with a chopping blade and pulse five to eight times or until the meat is minced. Set aside.

3. In a saucepan boil the potatoes in salted water until very tender (about 15 minutes depending on the size of the cubes). Drain them and mash thoroughly with a potato masher until no chunks remain. Set aside.

4. In a nonstick frying pan, heat the oil and sauté the onion until nicely browned. Add the garlic, ginger, and green chili and fry for 1 minute. Stir in the ground masala and salt and fry briefly. Finally add the meat and stir constantly over medium-

high heat until all the pink color disappears. Remove from the heat and cool slightly.

5. Add the lime juice, cilantro, and mashed potatoes and blend the mixture with your hands until it becomes a smooth dense ball.

6. To form the samosas, roll out the golf-ball-size balls of dough with a rolling pin into 6-inch disks about $1/16$ inch thick. Cut the disks in half and form a cone by folding the cut edge in half and pinching the edges together to seal tightly. Fill the cone with a tablespoon of the filling and pinch together the top edges to seal them closed. Be sure there are no holes or the filling will spill when fried. Repeat with the rest of the dough.

7. Heat 2 to 3 inches of vegetable oil in a wok to about 350 degrees F. Test by taking a tiny piece of dough and dropping it in the oil. If it immediately rises to the surface the oil is hot enough. Fry four or five at a time, turning frequently until they turn deep golden brown (3 to 5 minutes). If they brown too quickly, reduce the heat. Drain them on paper towels and serve warm.

PREPARATION TIME: 1 HOUR
FRYING TIME: 25 MINUTES
SERVES: 8 TO 10
YIELD: 30
RECIPE MAY BE PREPARED IN ADVANCE THROUGH STEP 6.

Beet Thoren, Fish Curry   Pullao w/ onions

DOSA

48

Roll #
32 02

Adda prep

45

46

Vegetables

This chapter is divided into two sections—dry and wet—
because the distinction between these types of vegetable
curries is significant in Kerala. Meals are composed
according to a balance of textures as well as flavors. The
goal is to avoid too much of the same consistency on the
plate. A guideline for putting together a meal with rice is
to choose one dry vegetable, one wet vegetable, a dhal,
and a fish, poultry, or meat dish. Or for a vegetarian meal,
choose a variety of wet and dry vegetables—some with
coconut, some without—and serve them with rice, dhal,
and *pappadam* (crisp legume wafers, page 219).

A key difference in these two vegetable categories is
the way in which each is seasoned with the trademark
flavorings of Kerala cuisine: mustard seeds, dried red
chilies, and fresh curry leaves. For dry stir-fries, the rule is
to fry these spices in hot oil first, then add the other ingredients to the flavored oil. Curries with a gravy are usually

The author and her aunt cooking in Kottayam.

given a seasoning as a last step, either by pouring the seasoned oil over the finished curry, or by spooning coconut oil and sprinkling fresh curry leaves over the dish before serving. These principles apply to meat and fish curries as well as vegetables.

The Hindu community in Kerala is considered the most skilled at making vegetable curries. Their repertoire is vast and can be best appreciated at a wedding or holiday feast where a vegetarian meal consists of at least a dozen vegetable preparations with rice, served on individual banana-leaf plates. For every dish there is a standard for how each vegetable should be cut: shreds, cubes, slivers, or matchsticks, and any deviation from tradition would make the dish unrecognizable to a local. For this reason I give precise specifications about the size and shape of the ingredients in these recipes.

Many people, like my aunt, have gardens in their compounds where they grow small gourds, squashes, beans, and curry leaves. And nearly every home has a steady supply of bananas, coconuts, and mangoes from the trees around them. Cooking with ingredients such as freshly scraped coconut and curry leaves plucked from the bush, gives the food a vividness that can be hard to duplicate in the United States. I have tried, however, to find convenient and adequate substitutes, and to make adjustments to the seasoning so they are as interesting as the originals.

Dry Vegetable Curries

Spicy Fried Tomatoes (Tomato Fry)
Eggplant in Tamarind Sauce (Eggplant *Thiyal*)
Squash with Mustard Seeds (Squash *Oolarthiathu*)
Green Beans with Urad Dhal (Green Beans *Oolarthiathu*)
Okra Stuffed with Masala (Okra *Varathathu*)
Spinach with Coconut (Spinach *Thoren*)
Beets with Coconut (Beet *Thoren*)
Carrots with Coconut (Carrot *Thoren*)
Chickpeas with Onion (*Kadala*)
Mixed Vegetables with Chickpeas (*Kootu Curry*)
Peppery Chickpeas
Potatoes with Cabbage
Pumpkin with Toasted Coconut (Pumpkin *Erisheri*)

Wet Vegetable Curries

Tomato and Cucumber with Mustard Seeds
   (Tomato and Cucumber *Pachadi*)
Okra with Crushed Mustard Seeds (Okra *Pachadi*)
Pineapple with Crushed Mustard Seeds (Pineapple
   Pachadi)
Mixed Vegetables with Coconut and Tamarind (*Aviyal*)
Cucumber with Black-eyed Peas (*Olan*)
Vegetables in Fragrant Coconut Milk (White Stew)
Vegetables in Spiced Coconut Milk (Brown Stew)
Fried Eggplant in Yogurt Sauce (Eggplant *Kichadi*)
Fried Bitter Gourd in Yogurt Sauce (Bitter Gourd *Kichadi*)
Buttermilk with Mango (Mango *Pulisheri*)
Spiced Buttermilk Curry (*Moru Kachiathu*)
Coconut Milk and Shallot Sauce (*Sothy*)

Dry Vegetable Curries

Spicy Fried Tomatoes
(Tomato Fry)

1 1/2 teaspoons ground cumin

1/2 teaspoon crushed black peppercorns

1/4 teaspoon mustard seeds, crushed

1/4 teaspoon turmeric

1/4 teaspoon cayenne

1/2 teaspoon sugar

2 teaspoons salt

6 tablespoons vegetable oil

18 fresh curry leaves

2 cups sliced onions

1 1/2 teaspoons minced garlic

4 large firm tomatoes (2 pounds), sliced into 1/2-inch-thick cross sections

This dish has been my Aunty Ambika's favorite since she was a child. The dish is simply slices of seared tomatoes with fried onions and a nice peppery bite. Use firm tomatoes and fry the ingredients in three batches so the tomatoes hold their shape.

1. Combine the cumin, crushed peppercorns, crushed mustard seeds, turmeric, cayenne, sugar, and salt. Divide into three equal portions and set aside.

2. Using one third of the ingredients, prepare the first batch by heating 2 tablespoons of the vegetable oil in a 12-inch nonstick frying pan over medium-high heat. Toss in six curry leaves. After the leaves crackle for a few seconds, add 2/3 cup onion and fry until it turns light brown. Add 1/2 teaspoon of the garlic and fry for a few seconds. Add one of the spice portions and fry, stirring constantly for 1 minute.

3. Push the onion to the edge of the pan. Add one third of the tomato slices, making a single layer in the pan. Fry over medium-high heat until lightly browned, about 1 1/2 minutes, and turn over carefully. Spread the onion over the tomatoes. When the second side is browned, slide the tomatoes and onion onto a platter and cover.

4. Wipe the pan clean and repeat twice. Serve warm.

PREPARATION TIME: 30 MINUTES

SERVES: 6

RECIPE MAY BE PREPARED AN HOUR IN ADVANCE IF KEPT COVERED.

Eggplant in Tamarind Sauce
(Eggplant *Thiyal*)

1/2 cup grated unsweetened coconut

Ground masala
- 4 teaspoons coriander
- 1/2 teaspoon cumin
- 1/2 teaspoon cayenne
- 1/4 teaspoon turmeric

1/2 teaspoon tamarind concentrate

3 cups (1 1/2 x 1/2-inch matchsticks) Japanese or Italian eggplant

6 tablespoons vegetable oil

1 1/2 cups sliced onions

1 fresh green chili (serrano or Thai), split lengthwise

1 1/2 teaspoons salt

1 teaspoon mustard seeds

2 dried red chilies

10 to 12 fresh curry leaves

This is an intensely flavored side dish with an underlying hint of sweetness. *Thiyals*, one of the Hindu specialties of Kerala, are characterized by their combination of tart tamarind and deeply toasted coconut.

1. In a frying pan, toast the coconut over medium heat, stirring constantly until it turns cinnamon brown and no white remains. Add the ground masala and continue toasting together over medium heat until the spices give off their aroma. Do not burn the coconut.

2. Place the coconut and spices in a blender with 1/2 cup water or more and process to form a finely ground paste, like a thick pesto. Set aside.

3. In a small bowl combine the tamarind concentrate with 2 tablespoons of hot water. Rub with your fingers to dissolve. Set aside.

4. In a wide nonstick skillet fry the eggplant in 3 tablespoons of the oil until it browns and softens and the eggplant releases its liquid (about 10 minutes). Remove the eggplant pieces to a plate, leaving behind any oil. Add another tablespoon of oil and fry the onions and green chili over medium-high heat until the onion is browned.

5. Return the eggplant to the frying pan and add the coconut paste and dissolved tamarind. Stir in the salt and 3/4 to 1 cup water, and cook until the eggplant is very soft (10 minutes). It should look like pieces of eggplant in a thick sauce. Add more

water as needed to maintain the proper consistency. Cover and remove from heat.

6. In a small frying pan, heat the remaining 2 tablespoons of oil over medium-high heat. Add the mustard seeds and cover. When the mustard seeds have popped add the dried red chilies and curry leaves. After the leaves crackle for a few seconds, pour the mixture over the cooked eggplant and stir.

PREPARATION TIME: 1 HOUR

SERVES: 6

RECIPE MAY BE PREPARED IN ADVANCE AND REHEATED.

Squash with Mustard Seeds
(Squash *Oolarthiathu*)

1¹/₂ pounds yellow squash and
    zucchini
¹/₄ teaspoon turmeric
¹/₄ teaspoon cayenne
³/₄ teaspoon salt
2 tablespoons vegetable oil
1 teaspoon mustard seeds
1 dried red chili
12 fresh curry leaves

In Kerala, the most basic way to prepare vegetables is to steam them in a little water with turmeric, cayenne, and salt, then fry them in oil seasoned with mustard seeds. It's a simple and flavorful technique, and I find it adapts well to yellow squash and zucchini.

1. Cut the yellow squash and zucchini into ¹/₂-inch dice, and place in a 2-quart saucepan with the turmeric, cayenne, salt, and 2 tablespoons water. Bring to a boil, reduce the heat to medium-low, cover and steam for 5 minutes or until the vegetables are just tender. Stir the vegetables occasionally as they steam. Drain.

2. In a deep nonstick pan or a wok heat the oil over medium-high heat. Add the mustard seeds and cover. When the mustard seeds pop, add the dried red chili and curry leaves and fry briefly. Add the drained vegetables and stir-fry until tender but not mushy. Taste for salt.

PREPARATION TIME: 25 MINUTES
SERVES: 6
RECIPE MAY BE PREPARED IN ADVANCE AND REHEATED.

Green Beans with Urad Dhal
(Green Beans *Oolarthiathu*)

1 pound fresh green beans

2 tablespoons vegetable oil

3/4 teaspoon mustard seeds

1 dried red chili

8 to 10 fresh curry leaves (optional)

1 tablespoon split urad dhal

1/3 cup finely chopped onion

1 teaspoon salt

2 tablespoons grated unsweetened
   coconut (optional)

This easy stir-fry has crunchy bits of fried urad dhal.

1. Wash and trim the beans and cut them into 3/4-inch lengths (about 3 cups). Set aside.

2. Heat the oil in a wok or nonstick pan over medium-high heat. Add the mustard seeds and cover. When the mustard seeds have popped toss in the dried red chili and curry leaves. After a few seconds, add the urad dhal and stir until the dhal turns pale gold. Add the onion and continue stirring until the dhal turns light brown and the onion becomes soft.

3. Put in the green beans, salt, and 1 tablespoon water and stir over medium heat for 10 minutes. If the beans get too dry, sprinkle on a teaspoon or two of water. While the beans are still a little crunchy, add the coconut. Continue stirring for another 5 minutes, or until the beans are tender.

PREPARATION TIME: 25 MINUTES

SERVES: 6

RECIPE MAY BE PREPARED IN ADVANCE AND REHEATED.

Okra Stuffed with Masala
(Okra *Varathathu*)

1 pound fresh okra

Ground masala
- 4 teaspoons coriander
- 2 teaspoons cumin
- 1/4 teaspoon cayenne
- 1/4 teaspoon black pepper
- 1/4 teaspoon turmeric

1 teaspoon salt

2 teaspoons fresh lemon juice

4 tablespoons vegetable oil

This is my grandmother's recipe for "stuffed lady's fingers" as she called it. I recommend filling them in advance and frying them just before serving.

1. Wash the okra and dry it thoroughly. Trim the stems down to 1/4 inch. Slit each piece of okra lengthwise, starting 1/4 inch from the cap and going all the way to the tip.

2. In a small bowl combine the ground masala, salt, lemon juice, and 1 tablespoon of the vegetable oil to make a paste. Using a butter knife, smear about 1/4 teaspoon of the paste into the slit in each okra. Set aside on a plate.

3. In a 12-inch nonstick frying pan wide enough to hold all the okra in a single layer heat the remaining 3 tablespoons oil. Or if all the okra won't fit, fry it in two batches using half the oil. Add the okra pieces and fry on medium heat. Turn the pieces occasionally until browned on all sides and tender (10 to 15 minutes).

PREPARATION TIME: 40 TO 50 MINUTES

SERVES: 6

RECIPE MAY BE PREPARED IN ADVANCE AND REHEATED.

Spinach with Coconut
(Spinach *Thoren*)

28 ounces fresh spinach or
  2 (10 ounce) packages frozen
  chopped spinach, thawed
3/4 cup grated unsweetened coconut
Ground masala
- 1/2 teaspoon cumin
- 1/8 teaspoon cayenne
- 1/8 teaspoon turmeric

1 teaspoon salt
1 fresh green chili (serrano or Thai),
  split lengthwise
2 tablespoons vegetable oil
1 teaspoon mustard seeds
2 dried red chilies
10 to 12 fresh curry leaves (optional)
1 cup finely chopped shallots or onion

Thoren is a type of stir-fry with shredded coconut, cooked in oil seasoned with mustard seeds, dried red chilies, and fresh curry leaves. It can be made with nearly any shredded vegetable. This one is delicious with fresh or frozen spinach.

1. Wash and dry fresh spinach, and chop finely, or drain the thawed spinach. Set aside.

2. In a bowl combine coconut, ground masala, salt, and green chili with enough water (about 1/4 cup) to make a thick paste. Set aside.

3. In a wok or large skillet heat the oil over medium-high heat. Add the mustard seeds and when they begin to pop toss in the dried chilies, curry leaves, and shallots and fry for 2 minutes or until the shallots begin to soften but not brown. Add the spinach and cook, stirring constantly until spinach is half cooked (about 5 minutes). Stir in the coconut paste and continue cooking, stirring constantly for another 5 minutes or until the spinach is tender. Remove from the heat and taste for salt. This curry is something like a moist stir-fry.

PREPARATION TIME: 25 MINUTES
SERVES: 6
RECIPE MAY BE PREPARED IN ADVANCE AND REHEATED.

Beets with Coconut
(Beet *Thoren*)

4 fresh medium beets (about 1
  pound)

3/4 cup grated unsweetened coconut

2 garlic cloves, crushed

1 fresh green chili, split lengthwise

Ground masala
- 1 teaspoon cumin
- 1/4 teaspoon cayenne
- 1/4 teaspoon turmeric

1 teaspoon salt

2 tablespoons vegetable oil

1 teaspoon mustard seeds

2 dried red chilies

10 to 12 fresh curry leaves

1 tablespoon uncooked long-grain
  rice

Beets and coconut make a nice combination in this dry curry that is a favorite at my aunt's house. As with any *thoren*, it's best to have each of the ingredients prepared and measured because they are added in rapid succession.

1. Peel the beets and grate them using a food processor fitted with the coarse shredding disk, or on the coarse side of a box grater. Set aside.

2. In a bowl combine the coconut, garlic, green chili, ground masala, and salt with about 1/4 cup water to form a moist ball. Set aside.

3. In a large wok heat the oil over medium-high heat. Add the mustard seeds and cover. When the seeds have popped toss in the dried red chilies and curry leaves. After the leaves crackle for a few seconds, put in the rice and stir for 5 seconds or until rice turns opaque white. Add the grated beets and stir thoroughly. Reduce the heat to medium, and cook, stirring occasionally until the beets become soft. Add the coconut mixture and continue cooking for another 5 minutes. Remove from the heat and check the salt.

PREPARATION TIME: 35 MINUTES

SERVES: 6

RECIPE MAY BE PREPARED IN ADVANCE AND REHEATED.

Carrots with Coconut
(Carrot *Thoren*)

1 pound carrots, peeled
³/₄ cup grated unsweetened coconut
³/₄ teaspoon cumin seed, finely
   ground with a mortar and pestle or
   coffee grinder
¹/₄ teaspoon cayenne
¹/₄ teaspoon turmeric
2 tablespoons vegetable oil
1 teaspoon mustard seeds
1 dried red chili
10 to 12 fresh curry leaves
1 tablespoon urad dhal
1 cup diced (¹/₂ inch) onion
1 ¹/₂ teaspoons salt

Another version of the classic Kerala stir-fry called *thoren*. Onions add a little body to this one, and my aunt warns not to let the carrots get too soft. It has the best texture when it's prepared just prior to serving.

1. Using a food processor or box grater, coarsely grate the carrots. Set aside.

2. In a bowl combine the coconut, ground cumin seeds, cayenne, turmeric, and about ¹/₄ cup water to form a moist ball. Set aside.

3. In a wok, heat the oil over medium-high heat. Add the mustard seeds and cover. When seeds begin to pop, toss in the dried red chili, curry leaves, and urad dhal and stir. When the urad dhal turns light brown, add the onion and fry until it softens and turns translucent, but not brown.

4. Add the grated carrots and salt, and stir frequently over medium-high heat. When the carrots are soft but still crunchy (2 to 3 minutes), add the coconut mixture and continue stirring for just another 2 to 3 minutes, until the carrots are tender but still orange, and the flavors are well blended. Do not overcook the carrots. Check the salt and serve immediately or the curry will become limp.

PREPARATION TIME: 35 MINUTES
SERVES: 6 TO 8
RECIPE SHOULD BE PREPARED JUST PRIOR TO SERVING.

Chickpeas with Onion
(*Kadala*)

6 tablespoons vegetable oil

1 teaspoon mustard seeds

1 dried red chili

10 to 12 fresh curry leaves

3 cups thinly sliced onions

Ground masala

- 2 teaspoons coriander
- 1 teaspoon cumin
- $1/4$ teaspoon cayenne
- $1/4$ teaspoon turmeric

1 teaspoon coarsely ground black pepper

1 teaspoon salt

2 (15-ounce) cans chickpeas, rinsed and drained ($3\,1/2$ cups)

$1/2$ cup Coconut Slices (page 220) (optional)

PREPARATION TIME: 35 MINUTES

SERVES: 6

RECIPE CAN BE PREPARED IN ADVANCE AND REHEATED.

In Kerala, black chickpeas are slow-cooked with lots of onions and slices of fresh coconut to make this thick, dark curry with a spicy bite. You can omit the sliced coconut to simplify this dish, but it does add nice texture. My aunt serves it for breakfast with a steamed cereal called *pootu*, but I suggest serving it for dinner with Shrimp in Coconut Milk (page 133), Squash with Mustard Seeds (page 72), and rice.

1. Heat the oil in a nonstick frying pan over medium-high heat; add the mustard seeds and cover. When the seeds pop, toss in the dried red chili and curry leaves. After the leaves crackle for a few seconds, put in the sliced onions and fry until the edges are nicely browned.

2. Add the ground masala, black pepper, and salt and stir for 1 minute or until the spices give off their aroma. Add a tablespoon or two of water to prevent sticking.

3. Add the chickpeas and coconut slices and continue to fry over medium heat, stirring frequently. As the mixture dries out, add water, a few tablespoons at a time, while continuing to stir. After 10 minutes the mixture should appear darker, and the chickpeas will begin to break down and blend with the onions. If the chickpeas have not broken down, break some up with pressure from your utensil. The final texture should be thick and pasty with some whole chickpeas remaining. Remove from the heat and taste for salt.

Mixed Vegetables with Chickpeas
(*Kootu* Curry)

1¹/₄ cups grated unsweetened
  coconut

³/₄ teaspoon black peppercorns,
  crushed with a mortar and pestle

Ground masala
- 2 teaspoons cumin
- ¹/₄ teaspoon cayenne
- ¹/₄ teaspoon turmeric

20 fresh curry leaves

2 cups cubed (¹/₂-inch) peeled boiling
  potatoes

1 cup cubed (¹/₂-inch) eggplant

¹/₄ teaspoon cayenne

¹/₈ teaspoon turmeric

1 teaspoon salt

1 cup canned chickpeas, rinsed and
  drained

1 cup cubed (¹/₂-inch) peeled, seeded
  cucumber

2 tablespoons vegetable oil

¹/₂ teaspoon mustard seeds

2 dried red chilies

PREPARATION TIME: 45 MINUTES
SERVES: 6 TO 8
RECIPE MAY BE PREPARED IN
  ADVANCE AND REHEATED.

A classic Kerala curry, with a thick, flavorful grated coconut sauce, particularly nice on a winter menu.

1. In a blender or food processor, combine ³/₄ cup of the coconut, the black pepper, and the ground masala. Add enough water (¹/₂ to ³/₄ cup) to process to a coarse paste, like thick pesto. Put in 10 of the curry leaves and process briefly to break up the leaves. Set the coconut paste aside.

2. In a large saucepan combine the potatoes, eggplant, cayenne, turmeric, and salt, with 1 cup water. Bring to a boil, reduce the heat, and simmer until vegetables are barely tender (5 to 7 minutes). Add the chickpeas, cucumber, and ¹/₂ cup water and continue simmering for another 5 minutes, until the cucumber becomes translucent and the vegetables are tender.

3. Stir in the coconut paste and bring to a boil, adding a little water as needed to keep the mixture from drying out. Simmer for 2 minutes and remove from the heat.

4. In a wok or frying pan, heat the oil. Add the mustard seeds and cover. After the seeds pop for a few seconds toss in the dried red chilies. Add the remaining ¹/₂ cup grated coconut and stir constantly over medium-high heat until the coconut turns light brown and very little white remains. Put in the remaining 10 curry leaves and stir briefly.

5. Mix the toasted coconut into the vegetables and stir over medium-low heat until the mixture is hot. Remove from the heat and taste for salt. This is a thick curry.

Peppery Chickpeas

4 tablespoons vegetable oil

2 cups finely chopped onions

Ground masala

- 2 teaspoons coriander
- 1 teaspoon cumin
- $^1/_4$ teaspoon cayenne
- $^1/_4$ teaspoon turmeric

2 (15-ounce) cans chickpeas, rinsed and drained (3 $^1/_2$ cups)

1 teaspoon coarsely ground black pepper

$^3/_4$ teaspoon salt

1 teaspoon fresh lemon juice

$^1/_4$ cup chopped fresh cilantro for garnish

My father created this simple yet delicious preparation for canned chickpeas. Black pepper, a spice native to Kerala, gives it just the right amount of spark, and we strongly prefer coarsely ground pepper (not preground) for this one.

1. Heat the oil in a nonstick frying pan over medium-high heat and sauté the onions until light brown. Add the ground masala and stir for 1 minute or until the spices give off their aroma.

2. Add the drained chickpeas, pepper, salt, and about a tablespoon of water. Fry over medium heat, stirring constantly until a few of the chickpeas begin to break down. Add a teaspoon of water at a time if it becomes dry. The curry will have no sauce but it should be moist.

3. Stir in the lemon juice, remove from the heat, and taste for salt. Garnish with the chopped cilantro.

PREPARATION TIME: 25 MINUTES

SERVES: 6

RECIPE MAY BE PREPARED IN ADVANCE THROUGH STEP 2; HOWEVER, WHEN REHEATING IT, ADD A LITTLE WATER TO KEEP THE CHICKPEAS MOIST.

Potatoes with Cabbage

4 medium boiling potatoes, peeled
  and cut into $1/2$-inch cubes
3 tablespoons vegetable oil
$3/4$ teaspoon mustard seeds
$1/2$ teaspoon cumin seeds
2 dried red chilies
10 curry leaves (optional)
$1/2$ head medium green cabbage,
  chopped medium fine (4 cups)

Ground masala
  • 2 teaspoons coriander
  • $1/4$ teaspoon turmeric
  • $1/8$ teaspoon cayenne
$1 1/4$ teaspoons salt

My grandmother's recipe is flavorful as well as pretty, with yellow potatoes, green cabbage, and black mustard seeds.

1. Boil the potatoes in salted water for 8 to 10 minutes or until they are barely tender; drain and set aside.

2. In a large wok, heat the oil over medium-high heat. Add the mustard seeds and cumin seeds and cover. When the mustard seeds begin to pop, toss in the dried red chilies and curry leaves and fry for a few seconds. Add the potatoes, cabbage, ground masala, and salt. Sprinkle 1 tablespoon water over the mixture and stir until thoroughly combined.

3. Stir constantly over medium heat until the cabbage and potatoes are completely tender, about 8 minutes. If the spices begin to stick to the pan, sprinkle with a little more water, but not enough to collect in the bottom of the pan. While stirring, you can break up the potatoes for a softer texture. Remove from the heat; taste for salt.

PREPARATION TIME: 40 MINUTES
SERVES: 6
RECIPE MAY BE PREPARED IN ADVANCE AND REHEATED.

Pumpkin with Toasted Coconut
(Pumpkin *Erisheri*)

$^1/_2$ cup whole mung beans

1 medium pumpkin or butternut
squash

1 cup grated unsweetened coconut

$^1/_2$ teaspoon chopped garlic

Ground masala
- 1 teaspoon cumin
- $^1/_2$ teaspoon cayenne
- $^1/_4$ teaspoon turmeric

$^1/_4$ teaspoon turmeric

$^1/_8$ teaspoon cayenne

1 $^1/_4$ teaspoons salt

2 tablespoons vegetable oil

1 teaspoon mustard seeds

2 dried red chilies

Pumpkins are used in curries in Kerala at various stages of ripeness. As a green vegetable they are used in spicy dishes like *sambar*, a pungent legume stew. But when they ripen they are made into sweeter dishes like this thick curry with toasted coconut and mung beans called *erisheri*. Butternut squash is also delicious prepared this way. This curry goes well with Green Beans with Urad Dhal (page 73), Chicken with Potato and Fennel Seeds (page 141), and rice.

1. In a dry frying pan, toast the mung beans over medium-high heat, stirring constantly until they begin to brown. Remove them to a strainer or fine colander and wash them briefly under running water; drain. Place the beans in a saucepan with 1 $^1/_2$ cups water and bring to a boil. Cover, reduce the heat to low, and simmer 20 minutes or until just tender.

2. Peel the pumpkin (or squash) and remove the seeds. Cut into $^3/_4$-inch cubes and measure 4 cups, reserving any extra for another use. Set aside.

3. Put $^3/_4$ cup of the coconut, the garlic, and the ground masala in a blender or food processor. Add $^1/_2$ cup water or more and process the mixture to the consistency of thick pesto. Set aside.

4. In a wide deep pan combine the pumpkin (or squash), turmeric, cayenne, salt, and 1 $^1/_2$ cups water. Bring to a boil, reduce the heat, and simmer, covered, until the pumpkin is tender and begins to break up when stirred (20 to 25 minutes).

Add the cooked mung beans and the coconut paste and stir to combine. Bring to a boil, then remove from the heat.

5. In a frying pan, heat the oil over medium-high heat. Add the mustard seeds and cover. When the seeds pop, toss in the dried red chilies and fry for a few seconds. Add the remaining $1/4$ cup of coconut and stir constantly over medium-high heat until the coconut turns cinnamon brown and no white remains. Stir this into the cooked vegetables and heat the mixture until warmed through, adding more water if it dries out. Remove from the heat and check the salt. The curry should appear as chunks of pumpkin with a thick sauce.

PREPARATION TIME: 1 HOUR

SERVES: 6

RECIPE MAY BE PREPARED IN ADVANCE AND REHEATED.

Wet Vegetable Curries

Tomato and Cucumber with Mustard Seeds
(Tomato and Cucumber *Pachadi*)

2 cucumbers or 1 English cucumber

3 large tomatoes, seeded

$1/2$ teaspoon ground cumin

1 teaspoon salt

1 fresh green chili (serrano or Thai),
   split lengthwise

$2/3$ cup plain yogurt

2 tablespoons vegetable oil

1 teaspoon mustard seeds

2 dried red chilies

10 to 12 fresh curry leaves

Pachadis are lively, light vegetable preparations with mustard seeds and a yogurt sauce. This recipe has been in my family for years, and it's one of my favorites.

1. Peel the cucumbers, quarter them lengthwise, and remove the seeds. Then slice the quarters crosswise into $1/8$-inch-thick pieces (about 2 cups). Cut the seeded tomatoes into small pieces approximately the same size as the cucumber (about 2 cups). Place the cucumber, tomato, cumin, salt, green chili, and $1/4$ cup water in a wide deep pan. Bring to a boil, reduce the heat, and simmer until the cucumber looks glassy (about 10 minutes). Remove from the heat. Stir in the yogurt and combine thoroughly.

2. In a small covered frying pan, heat the oil over medium-high heat. Add the mustard seeds and cover. When the seeds have popped for a few seconds, toss in the dried red chilies and curry leaves and fry for a few seconds. Pour the mixture into the vegetables, and stir to combine. The curry should be the consistency of a thick sauce.

PREPARATION TIME: 25 MINUTES

SERVES: 6

RECIPE MAY BE PREPARED IN ADVANCE AND GENTLY REHEATED, BEING
   CAREFUL NOT TO CURDLE THE YOGURT.

Okra with Crushed Mustard Seeds
(Okra *Pachadi*)

1 pound fresh okra
Vegetable oil for deep-frying, plus 2
   tablespoons
1 cup thinly sliced onion
2 fresh green chilies (serrano or Thai),
   split lengthwise
1 teaspoon ground cumin
$^1/_4$ teaspoon cayenne
1 teaspoon salt
2 cups plain yogurt
$^1/_2$ teaspoon mustard seeds, crushed
   with a mortar and pestle

Here is another version of *pachadi*, a popular vegetable preparation in Kerala. Be sure to add the crisply fried okra to the yogurt just before serving so it doesn't become soggy.

1. Trim the okra and slice it into $^1/_8$-inch rounds. In a small wok, heat the oil for deep-frying on medium-high. Deep-fry the okra until the pieces are crisp and brown but the skin remains green (10 to 15 minutes); stir constantly. Spread the okra on a paper towel and set aside.
2. In the same pan, wiped clean, heat 2 tablespoons oil. Add the onion and green chilies and fry until the onion becomes soft but not brown. Add the cumin, cayenne, and salt and fry 2 to 3 minutes. Remove from the heat. Add the yogurt and crushed mustard seeds and combine thoroughly. It should be a moderately thick sauce, not runny.
3. Before serving, add the okra to the yogurt mixture and gently stir. Taste for salt and serve immediately.

PREPARATION TIME: 40 MINUTES
SERVES: 6
RECIPE MAY BE PREPARED IN ADVANCE THROUGH STEP 2.

Pineapple with Crushed Mustard Seeds
(Pineapple *Pachadi*)

2 cups cubed ($^1/_2$-inch) fresh
   pineapple
$^1/_2$ teaspoon turmeric
$^1/_2$ teaspoon salt
1 cup grated unsweetened coconut
1 teaspoon ground cumin
$^1/_4$ teaspoon cayenne
2 tablespoons vegetable oil
$^1/_2$ teaspoon whole mustard seeds,
   plus $^1/_2$ teaspoon mustard seeds
   crushed with a mortar and pestle
2 dried red chilies
10 to 12 curry leaves

A sweet and hot side dish, this is typically served as part of the feast for *Onam*, Kerala's fall harvest festival. It's also nice with dry meat curries like Minced Beef with Coconut (page 152) or Spicy Beef Curry (page 153) and Okra Stuffed with Masala (page 74) plus dhal and rice.

1. In a saucepan, bring the pineapple, turmeric, and $^1/_2$ cup water to a boil. Reduce to a simmer and cook until the pineapple is tender but not mushy. Remove from the heat, and stir in the salt.

2. Process the coconut, cumin, cayenne, and $^3/_4$ cup water in a blender or food processor until it is the consistency of thick pesto. Set aside.

3. In a frying pan heat the oil. Add $^1/_2$ teaspoon (whole) mustard seeds and cover. When the seeds pop, toss in the dried red chilies and curry leaves. After the leaves crackle for a few seconds, add the coconut paste and fry for a minute. Pour this mixture into the cooked pineapple and combine thoroughly. The mixture should be thick.

4. Heat the pineapple over medium-low heat until warmed through. Add the $^1/_2$ teaspoon of crushed mustard seeds and remove from the heat. Taste for salt.

PREPARATION TIME: 30 MINUTES
SERVES: 6
RECIPE MAY BE PREPARED IN ADVANCE AND REHEATED.

Mixed Vegetables with Coconut and Tamarind
(*Aviyal*)

$^1/_2$ teaspoon tamarind concentrate

1 cup grated unsweetened coconut

$^1/_4$ cup chopped onion

Ground masala

- $^1/_4$ teaspoons cumin
- $^1/_8$ teaspoon cayenne
- $^1/_8$ teaspoon turmeric

1 large peeled boiling potato

2 peeled carrots

1 small zucchini

12 fresh green beans

2 fresh green chilies (serrano or Thai), split lengthwise

$1^1/_2$ teaspoons salt

$^1/_4$ teaspoon cayenne

$^1/_4$ teaspoon turmeric

1 small peeled, seeded cucumber

$^1/_2$ cup frozen peas

15 to 18 fresh curry leaves

1 tablespoon coconut oil (optional)

PREPARATION TIME: 40 MINUTES

SERVES: 6 TO 8

RECIPE MAY BE PREPARED IN ADVANCE AND REHEATED.

Aviyal, one of the classic curries of the Hindu community in Kerala, is made with many different vegetables cut into matchsticks cooked in a coconut and tamarind sauce. This dish is an essential part of every Hindu wedding and holiday feast.

1. In a small bowl combine the tamarind with $^1/_4$ cup hot water. Using your fingers, thoroughly break up the tamarind. Set aside.

2. In a blender or food processor combine the coconut, onion, and ground masala with $^3/_4$ cup water (or more) and process to the consistency of thick pesto.

3. Cut the potatoes, carrots, and zucchini into 2 x $^1/_2$-inch matchsticks. Cut the green beans into $1^1/_2$-inch lengths. Combine the cut vegetables, green chilies, salt, cayenne, and turmeric with 1 cup water in a deep pot and bring to a boil. Boil the vegetables for 5 minutes. Meanwhile, cut the cucumber into 2 x $^1/_2$-inch matchsticks. Add the cucumber, peas, and the tamarind juice; boil for another minute.

4. Stir the coconut mixture into the cooked vegetables, turn the heat down to medium, and simmer until the vegetables are completely cooked and the sauce is thick (5 to 10 minutes). Add more water if the mixture gets too thick to simmer.

5. Sprinkle in the curry leaves and coconut oil. Simmer for another minute and remove from the heat.

Cucumber with Black-eyed Peas
(*Olan*)

2 peeled, seeded cucumbers or
  1 seeded English cucumber
$^1/_2$ cup canned coconut milk
$^2/_3$ cup drained canned black-eyed
  peas
2 fresh green chilies (serrano or Thai),
  split lengthwise
10 fresh curry leaves
$^1/_2$ teaspoon salt
2 teaspoons coconut oil

This delightfully simple coconut milk curry has the tropical flavors that make Kerala curries distinctive. I learned it from my aunt, and it's one of my favorite dishes. Aunty often makes it with a vegetable called ash gourd (winter melon) but cucumber is a good substitute. In Kerala it's always eaten with a sour buttermilk curry; serve it with Buttermilk with Mango (page 97), Eggplant in Tamarind Sauce (page 70), Fragrant Chicken Stir-Fry (page 140), and rice.

1. Cut the cucumber into $^1/_2$ x $^1/_2$ x $^1/_8$ -inch pieces. Combine the cucumber with $^1/_4$ cup of the coconut milk, the drained black-eyed peas, green chilies, curry leaves, salt, and $^1/_4$ cup water in a 2-quart saucepan. Bring to a boil, and simmer, uncovered, until the cucumber becomes translucent (about 8 minutes).
2. Add the remaining $^1/_4$ cup coconut milk and heat through but do not boil. Remove from the heat.
3. Add the coconut oil and stir briefly.

> PREPARATION TIME: 25 MINUTES
> SERVES: 6
> THIS RECIPE MAY BE PREPARED IN ADVANCE AND GENTLY REHEATED, BEING CAREFUL NOT TO BOIL THE COCONUT MILK OR IT WILL CURDLE.

Vegetables in Fragrant Coconut Milk
(White Stew)

2 peeled boiling potatoes

2 peeled carrots

1 1/2 cups thinly sliced onions

1 to 2 fresh green chilies (serrano or Thai), split lengthwise

10 thin slices ginger

16 to 20 fresh curry leaves

1 teaspoon salt

3/4 cup canned coconut milk

1 cup frozen peas

1 tablespoon coconut oil (optional)

Called "white stew," this dish is delicately flavored with green chili and ginger, but it is the fresh curry leaves that really make it come alive. In a Hindu home this meatless stew would accompany Lacy Rice Pancakes (page 50) or Fresh Rice Noodles (page 52); it's also tasty with rice and other curries.

1. Cut the potatoes into 1/2-inch cubes. Cut the carrots into 2-inch matchsticks. Combine the potatoes, carrots, onions, chilies, ginger, half the curry leaves, salt, 1/2 cup of the coconut milk, and 1 1/2 cups water in a 2-quart saucepan. Bring to a boil, reduce the heat and simmer, uncovered, for 15 minutes, or until the potatoes are tender. Break up some of the potato pieces with the back of a spoon to thicken the sauce.

2. Add the peas and simmer 5 minutes, until cooked through.

3. Stir in the remaining 1/4 cup coconut milk, bring just to a simmer, and remove from the heat. Taste for salt.

4. Sprinkle the remaining curry leaves and coconut oil over the curry and serve.

PREPARATION TIME: 30 MINUTES

SERVES: 6 TO 8

RECIPE MAY BE PREPARED IN ADVANCE AND GENTLY REHEATED, BEING CAREFUL NOT TO BOIL THE COCONUT MILK OR IT WILL CURDLE.

Vegetables in Spiced Coconut Milk
(Brown Stew)

2 peeled boiling potatoes

2 peeled carrots

$3/4$ cup sliced onion

2 fresh green chilies (serrano or Thai),
  split lengthwise

6 thin slices ginger

Ground masala

- 4 teaspoons coriander
- $1/2$ teaspoon cumin
- $1/4$ teaspoon cayenne
- $1/8$ teaspoon black pepper
- $1/8$ teaspoon turmeric

$1/4$ teaspoon fennel seeds, finely
  ground with a mortar and pestle or
  coffee grinder

1 (1-inch) piece cinnamon

3 whole cloves

$1^1/2$ teaspoons salt

1 cup cauliflower florets

$1/2$ cup cut-up green beans
  (1-inch lengths)

1 cup coconut milk

$1/2$ cup frozen peas

2 tablespoons vegetable oil

$1/2$ teaspoon mustard seeds

2 dried red chilies

12 to 18 fresh curry leaves

$1^1/2$ tablespoons finely chopped
  shallots or onion

"Brown stew" in Kerala is flavored with a ground spice masala that turns the coconut milk sauce light brown. This one makes a delicious first course with Lacy Rice Pancakes (page 50) or Coconut Rice Pancakes (page 56), or for a main course have it with rice and curries.

1. Cut the potatos and carrots into $1/2$-inch cubes. In a large pot combine the potatoes, carrots, onions, green chilies, ginger, ground masala, fennel, cinnamon stick, cloves, salt, and 1 cup water; bring to a boil. Reduce the heat, cover, and simmer until the vegetables are tender, about 10 minutes.

2. Add the cauliflower, beans, and $3/4$ cup of the coconut milk, cover, and continue cooking until the cauliflower is tender but not mushy, 5 to 10 minutes.

3. Add the peas and the remaining $1/4$ cup coconut milk and when it simmers remove from the heat. Set aside.

4. In a small frying pan, heat the oil over medium-high heat. Add the mustard seeds and cover. When the seeds pop, toss in the dried red chilies, curry leaves, and shallots and fry until the shallots brown. Pour the mixture over the vegetables and stir to combine. Taste for salt.

PREPARATION TIME: 45 MINUTES

SERVES: 6 TO 8

RECIPE MAY BE PREPARED IN ADVANCE AND GENTLY REHEATED, BEING CAREFUL NOT TO BOIL THE COCONUT MILK OR IT WILL CURDLE.

A Kochi warehouse piled high with sacks of pepper-corns.

Fried Eggplant in Yogurt Sauce
(Eggplant *Kichadi*)

1 cup grated unsweetened coconut

1/2 teaspoon mustard seeds, crushed
   with a mortar and pestle, plus
   1/2 teaspoon whole mustard seeds

14 to 18 fresh curry leaves

1 to 2 fresh green chilies (serrano or
   Thai), stemmed and split in half

4 1/2 tablespoons vegetable oil

1/2 pound Japanese eggplant, sliced
   into 1/4-inch-thick rounds

1 teaspoon salt

1 cup plain yogurt

1/4 teaspoon cumin seeds

1/4 teaspoon peppercorns, crushed
   with a mortar and pestle

1 dried red chili

Kichadi is a favorite vegetable curry in Hindu homes of Kerala. It combines a yogurt and coconut sauce with a fried vegetable such as eggplant, bitter gourd, or okra. Slender Japanese eggplants work best for this one.

1. Combine the coconut, 1/2 teaspoon crushed mustard seeds, 6 or 8 of the curry leaves, the split chilies, and up to 1 cup water, as needed, in a blender or food processor. Process until the mixture forms a paste like thick pesto.

2. In a wide nonstick (very important) frying pan, heat 1 1/2 tablespoons of the vegetable oil over medium heat. Fry half of the eggplant slices, or as many as the pan can hold in a single layer, over medium heat until browned on each side and tender inside. Remove to a plate lined with a paper towel; fry the remaining eggplant in an additional 1 1/2 tablespoons of oil. When all the eggplant is cooked, chop it into roughly 1/4-inch pieces. Sprinkle with 1/4 teaspoon salt; set aside.

3. Wipe clean the frying pan used for the eggplant. Add the coconut paste, 3/4 teaspoon salt, and 1/4 cup water. Simmer the mixture over low heat for 2 to 3 minutes, until lightly cooked. Mix in the yogurt, bring to a simmer, and immediately remove from the heat. Do not boil or the yogurt will curdle.

4. In a small covered frying pan heat the remaining 1 1/2 tablespoons vegetable oil over medium-high heat. Add 1/2 teaspoon whole mustard seeds and cover. When the seeds begin to pop, add the cumin seeds, peppercorns, and dried red

chili. After 5 to 10 seconds, when the cumin seeds have browned, toss in the remaining curry leaves. After the leaves crackle for a few seconds, pour the entire contents of the frying pan into the coconut and yogurt mixture and stir. Check the salt. Add the fried eggplant and gently fold in. It should be the consistency of very thick soup. Serve warm.

PREPARATION TIME: 45 MINUTES

SERVES: 6

RECIPE MAY BE PREPARED IN ADVANCE AND GENTLY REHEATED BEFORE SERVING, BEING CAREFUL NOT TO CURDLE THE YOGURT.

Fried Bitter Gourd in Yogurt Sauce
(Bitter Gourd *Kichadi*)

Bitter gourd has a strong, distinctive taste. Some people blanch the bitter gourd first to mellow its flavor, but I find it fries more easily when I skip that step.

Follow the directions for Fried Eggplant in Yogurt Sauce (page 94), except replace 1/2 pound eggplant with 3/4 to 1 pound bitter gourd. Quarter the gourd lengthwise, remove the tough seeds, and slice it into 1/4-inch or thinner pieces. Fry the pieces in a nonstick pan over medium heat, as with the eggplant, until lightly browned. Sprinkle with the salt according to the recipe and set aside. Proceed as with the previous recipe.

PREPARATION TIME: 45 MINUTES
SERVES: 6

Buttermilk with Mango
(Mango *Pulisheri*)

$^1/_2$ cup grated unsweetened coconut

Ground masala
- $^1/_4$ teaspoon cumin
- $^1/_4$ teaspoon cayenne
- $^1/_8$ teaspoon turmeric

$^1/_2$ ripe but firm large peeled mango

2 fresh green chilies (serrano or Thai), split lengthwise

$^1/_4$ teaspoon cayenne

$^1/_8$ teaspoon turmeric

1 teaspoon salt

2 cups buttermilk

$1^1/_2$ tablespoons vegetable oil

$^1/_2$ teaspoon mustard seeds

$^1/_4$ teaspoon fenugreek seeds

1 dried red chili

10 to 12 fresh curry leaves

PREPARATION TIME: 30 MINUTES
SERVES: 6 TO 8
RECIPE MAY BE PREPARED AN HOUR IN ADVANCE THROUGH STEP 3, OTHERWISE THE BUTTERMILK CURDLES AS IT SITS.

There are many buttermilk curries in Kerala, where the people have a particular fondness for sour things. This is the *Nayar* (Hindu) version my aunt makes, with chunks of sweet mango contrasting with the sour buttermilk. Pour this tangy sauce over rice instead of dhal, and serve with Beets with Coconut (page 76), Eggs with Spicy Masala (page 150), and Lamb *Vindaloo* (page 159).

1. In a blender combine the coconut, ground masala, and $^1/_2$ cup water. Process together to make a paste like thick pesto. Set aside.

2. Cut the mango into $^1/_2$-inch cubes (about 1 cup). In a saucepan combine the mango, green chilies, cayenne, turmeric, salt, and 1 cup water. Bring to a boil, reduce the heat, and simmer until the mango is soft when pierced with a knife.

3. Add the coconut paste and buttermilk and stir constantly over medium-high heat to prevent it from boiling and curdling. When the mixture is hot and a little steam is visible rising off the top, remove it from the heat and cover.

4. In a small frying pan heat the oil over medium-high heat. Add the mustard seeds and cover. After the seeds have popped for a few seconds, put in the fenugreek seeds and dried red chili. When the fenugreek seeds are lightly browned toss in the curry leaves. Let the leaves crackle for a few seconds, then pour the entire contents into the buttermilk. Check the salt, and serve warm, over rice.

Spiced Buttermilk Curry

(*Moru Kachiathu*)

3 cups buttermilk

Ground masala
- ¹/₂ teaspoon turmeric
- ¹/₄ teaspoon cumin
- ¹/₄ teaspoon cayenne

10 to 12 fresh curry leaves

10 thin slices ginger

3 fresh green chilies (serrano or Thai),
  split lengthwise

1 tablespoon fresh lime juice

³/₄ to 1 teaspoon salt

2 tablespoons vegetable oil

¹/₂ teaspoon mustard seeds

¹/₈ teaspoon fenugreek seeds

2 dried red chilies

¹/₄ cup finely chopped shallots or
  onion

This Syrian Christian buttermilk curry comes from Nimmy Paul, a cooking teacher in Kochi. It's essentially a thin sour soup seasoned with aromatics. A favorite combination among the Syrian Christians is this dish with plain rice and Fish with Red Sauce (page 128).

1. In a 2-quart saucepan combine the buttermilk, ground masala, curry leaves, ginger, green chilies, lime juice, and salt. Stir constantly over medium heat. Do not boil or the buttermilk will curdle. When the mixture is warmed through and a little steam is visible rising off the top, remove it from the heat and cover.

2. In a small frying pan heat the oil. Add the mustard seeds and cover. When mustard seeds begin to pop, put in the fenugreek seeds and dried red chilies and fry briefly. Then stir in the shallots and fry for 1 minute or until they just begin to brown. Pour into the buttermilk mixture and stir. Taste for salt and serve promptly.

PREPARATION TIME: 20 MINUTES

SERVES: 6 TO 8

RECIPE MAY BE PREPARED AN HOUR IN ADVANCE THROUGH STEP 1, OTHERWISE THE BUTTERMILK CURDLES AS IT SITS.

Coconut Milk and Shallot Sauce
(*Sothy*)

1 1/2 cups canned coconut milk
1/2 cup sliced shallots or onion
2 fresh green chilies (serrano or Thai),
    split lengthwise
14 to 18 fresh curry leaves
1/8 teaspoon turmeric
1/2 teaspoon salt
1 tablespoon vegetable oil
1/4 teaspoon mustard seeds
1 dried red chili
1 tablespoon fresh lime juice

Over 50 years ago my grandmother learned this dish from a Sri Lankan friend, and it's been a family favorite ever since. Although it isn't from Kerala, I couldn't help including it because it's so delicious and I eat it every time I visit there. It's an aromatic coconut milk sauce that my family eats with Fresh Rice Noodles (page 52). If you don't want to make the noodles from scratch you could use fresh or frozen rice noodles sold at Asian grocery stores. It's also quite tasty poured over Rice Noodle Stir-Fry (page 55).

1. In a 2- or 3-quart saucepan combine 1 cup of the coconut milk, the shallots, green chilies, 8 to 10 curry leaves, turmeric, salt, and 1 cup water. Simmer together until onions are soft and mixture is medium-thick, like tomato soup.
2. Add the remaining 1/2 cup coconut milk. Bring just up to a simmer, cover, and remove from heat.
3. In a small frying pan with a lid heat the oil, add the mustard seeds, and cover. When the seeds have popped toss in the dried red chili and the remaining curry leaves. After the leaves crackle for a few seconds, pour into the warm coconut milk mixture.
4. Stir in the lime juice and taste for salt.

PREPARATION TIME: 20 MINUTES
SERVES: 4 AS A LIGHT MEAL OR 6 AS A FIRST COURSE
RECIPE MAY BE PREPARED IN ADVANCE THROUGH STEP 3. REHEAT GENTLY
  BUT DO NOT BOIL.

Dhal

The word "dhal" is used in India to refer to any dried split or whole legume, as well as a cooked dish of seasoned legumes. Dhal provides a crucial source of protein in the Indian diet, particularly among the Hindus, who tend to consume less animal protein.

Cooked dhal is always served with rice and curries as part of what is called a "rice meal"—the largest meal of the day. In Kerala, meals are eaten with the right hand by forming the food into bites that can be picked up with the fingers. Dhal functions as the binder between the rice and curries, making this process easier. Without it the rice would fall from your fingers and some curries would be too liquid to pick up.

There is a rich variety of dhals in the Indian diet, but a great favorite in Kerala is a golden legume called thoor dhal: similar in appearance to yellow split peas, only flatter and smaller. This pleasant, earthy-tasting dhal is

Ground spices and aromatics, the heart of Kerala's curries.

good simmered with vegetables like tomatoes or bitter gourd, and it's almost always given a final seasoning of mustard seeds. Other dhals like mung and masoor are also enjoyed in Kerala for their distinctive flavors and textures, and recipes for them are included here as well.

Sambar and *rasam* are two other South Indian dishes with legumes as their base. *Sambar* is a thick stew with an assertive flavor, also eaten with rice; *rasam* is a pungent broth that is spooned over rice or drunk as a restorative beverage by people with head colds. At a Hindu wedding feast, there are multiple courses of rice and curries, each accompanied by a different dhal dish: first seasoned dhal, then *sambar*, and finally *rasam*.

Although an Indian dinner could be perfectly tasty without dhal, I like the way it rounds out the textures of a meal and provides contrast to the more intensely flavored curries on the plate. In this chapter you'll find a range of choices, all of which mix well with the other dishes in the book.

Seasoned Dhal

Mung Dhal with Coconut

Thoor Dhal with Tomato and Onion

Dhal with Fried Bitter Gourd

Masoor Dhal with Toasted Coriander

Spicy Dhal and Vegetable Stew (*Sambar*)

Spicy Dhal and Shallot Stew (Onion *Sambar*)

Dhal and Pepper Broth (Pepper *Rasam*)

Seasoned Dhal

1 cup thoor dhal, masoor dhal, or
   yellow split peas
2 tablespoons vegetable oil
$^1/_2$ teaspoon mustard seeds
1 dried red chili
10 fresh curry leaves (optional)
$^1/_2$ cup chopped onion
1 teaspoon minced garlic

Ground masala
  • $^1/_2$ teaspoon cumin
  • $^1/_4$ teaspoon turmeric
  • $^1/_8$ teaspoon cayenne
1 teaspoon salt
1 teaspoon fresh lemon juice
1 teaspoon Ghee (page 218)
   (optional)

Hindus have an infinite number of ways to flavor their daily dhal. This version is good for most split lentils, but it's best with thoor dhal, a flat golden legume favored for its sweet, earthy taste.

1. In a large bowl wash the dhal in several changes of water; drain. Place the dhal and $2^1/_2$ cups water in a 2-quart saucepan and bring to a boil. Reduce to a simmer and cook, partially covered, for 30 minutes (45 minutes for yellow split peas), or until the water is absorbed and the peas break up under pressure from the back of a spoon. Check to make sure it doesn't boil over.

2. When the dhal has finished cooking, heat the oil in a frying pan. Add the mustard seeds to the oil and heat until they pop. When the popping subsides, toss in the dried red chili and curry leaves. After a few seconds, add the onion and fry until light brown. Put in the garlic and fry 1 minute. Next, add the ground masala and fry for another minute. Stir this mixture into the dhal, along with $^1/_2$ cup water and the salt. Partially cover and continue simmering another 10 minutes, adding more water if the mixture is too thick. It should be the consistency of thick pea soup. Remove from the heat.

3. Stir in the lemon juice and ghee. Taste for salt.

PREPARATION TIME: 1 HOUR
SERVES: 6
RECIPE MAY BE PREPARED IN ADVANCE AND REHEATED.

Mung Dhal with Coconut

1 cup split mung dhal

3/4 cup grated unsweetened coconut

1 fresh green chili (serrano or Thai), stemmed

1/2 teaspoon cumin seeds, crushed with a mortar and pestle

1/4 teaspoon turmeric

6 to 8 fresh curry leaves (optional)

1 teaspoon salt

1 tablespoon coconut oil (optional)

This is a very simple but very good dhal that my aunt makes. Mung dhal is a small, round, pale yellow dhal and my aunt toasts it first to deepen the flavor.

1. In a large frying pan toast the mung dhal over medium-high heat, stirring frequently until it turns pale orange. Place in a strainer or fine colander and rinse thoroughly. Drain.

2. In a 2-quart saucepan combine the toasted dhal with 3 cups water and bring to a boil. Reduce the heat to low, partly cover, and simmer for 25 minutes, until soft. Check to make sure it doesn't boil over. Mash the cooked dhal a few times with a potato masher or the back of a spoon until the texture resembles thick soup.

3. Combine the coconut, green chili, crushed cumin seeds, turmeric, and curry leaves in a blender (or food processor), adding just enough water to form a paste like thick pesto.

4. Add the coconut mixture and salt to the cooked dhal, plus more water as needed to obtain the consistency of thick pea soup. Bring just to a boil and remove from the heat. Stir in the coconut oil and check the salt.

PREPARATION TIME: 45 MINUTES

SERVES: 6

RECIPE MAY BE PREPARED IN ADVANCE AND REHEATED.

Thoor Dhal with Tomato and Onion

1 cup thoor dhal or yellow split peas

¹/₄ teaspoon turmeric

¹/₂ cup sliced onion

2 fresh green chilies (serrano or Thai), split lengthwise (optional)

1 teaspoon minced garlic

1 teaspoon minced ginger

1 cup chopped tomato

1 to 1¹/₄ teaspoons salt

2 tablespoons vegetable oil

1 teaspoon mustard seeds

2 dried red chilies

10 to 12 fresh curry leaves

Adjust the green chilies to make this colorful, chunky dhal either spicy or mild.

1. In a large bowl wash the dhal in several changes of water; drain. Place the dhal, turmeric, and 2¹/₂ cups water in a 2-quart saucepan and bring to a boil. Reduce to a simmer and cook, partially covered, for 30 minutes (45 minutes for yellow split peas), or until the water has been absorbed and the peas break up under pressure from the back of a spoon. Check to make sure it doesn't boil over.

2. When the peas are soft, stir in the onion, green chilies, garlic, and ginger and simmer, uncovered, for 5 minutes or until the onions are soft. Add the tomato and salt and cook another 5 to 10 minutes until the tomatoes are cooked but not falling apart. Remove from the heat.

3. In a small frying pan heat the oil over medium-high heat. Add the mustard seeds and cover. When seeds have popped toss in the dried red chilies and curry leaves. After the leaves crackle for a few seconds, pour the contents into the dhal and stir to combine. The mixture should be the texture of thick pea soup. Taste for salt.

PREPARATION TIME: 50 MINUTES

SERVES: 6

RECIPE MAY BE PREPARED IN ADVANCE AND REHEATED.

Dhal with Fried Bitter Gourd

1 medium bitter gourd

1 cup thoor dhal or yellow split peas

2 tablespoons vegetable oil

1¼ teaspoons salt

3 teaspoons Sambar Powder
(page 222)

Bitter gourd is an acquired taste, but those who like it tend to like it passionately. Frying the vegetable to a crisp brown brings out the best flavor.

1. Quarter the bitter gourd, remove the seeds, and cut it into ¼-inch-thick slices (about 1 cup).

2. In a large bowl wash the dhal in several changes of water; drain. Bring the dhal and 2 ½ cups water to a boil in a 2-quart saucepan. Reduce the heat to low and simmer, partially covered, for 30 minutes (45 minutes for yellow split peas) or until the water is absorbed and the peas break under pressure from the back of a spoon. Check that it doesn't boil over.

3. In a nonstick frying pan sauté the bitter gourd in the oil until reddish brown. Remove to a paper towel and sprinkle with ¼ teaspoon of the salt. Set aside.

4. When the dhal is cooked, mash it up with a potato masher or the back of a spoon until most of the peas are broken down. Add the sambar powder and the remaining 1 teaspoon salt, and simmer for 5 minutes.

5. Stir in the bitter gourd and taste for salt. The consistency should be like thick pea soup. Remove from the heat. Serve warm.

PREPARATION TIME: 1 HOUR
SERVES: 6
RECIPE MAY BE PREPARED IN ADVANCE AND REHEATED.

Masoor Dhal with Toasted Coriander

1 cup masoor dhal
$1/4$ teaspoon turmeric
2 teaspoons ground coriander
$1/4$ cup grated unsweetened coconut
$1/8$ teaspoon cayenne
1 teaspoon salt
1 tablespoon vegetable oil
$1/4$ teaspoon mustard seeds
1 dried red chili
6 to 8 fresh curry leaves

These legumes appear coral-colored when raw, but turn yellow when cooked. Toasting the coriander and coconut adds a nice dimension to this dish.

1. Place the dhal in a bowl and rinse in several changes of cold water until the water no longer appears cloudy. Drain and place in a 2-quart saucepan with $2 1/2$ cups water and the turmeric. Bring to a boil, reduce the heat to low, and simmer, partially covered, for 20 to 25 minutes, or until the water has been absorbed and the dhal is completely soft. Check that it doesn't boil over.

2. Place the coriander in a dry frying pan and stir over medium heat for 5 minutes or until the spice gives off a toasted aroma. Set aside.

3. In the same pan, wiped clean, toast the coconut over medium-high heat until it turns cinnamon brown and no white remains. Set aside.

4. When the dhal is cooked, add the toasted coriander and coconut, cayenne, salt, and additional water if needed to achieve the consistency of pea soup. Continue simmering for another 5 minutes. Remove from the heat.

5. In a small frying pan heat the oil over medium-high heat. Add the mustard seeds and cover. When the seeds pop, toss in the dried red chili and curry leaves. After the curry leaves have crackled for a few seconds pour the mixture into the dhal. Stir and taste for salt.

PREPARATION TIME: 45 MINUTES
SERVES: 6
RECIPE MAY BE PREPARED IN
  ADVANCE AND REHEATED.

Spicy Dhal and Vegetable Stew
(Sambar)

1/2 cup thoor dhal or yellow split peas

1/8 teaspoon turmeric

1/4 teaspoon tamarind concentrate

2 tablespoons vegetable oil

1/8 teaspoon fenugreek seeds

1/8 teaspoon asafetida

1 cup cubed (3/4-inch) peeled boiling
  potato

1 cup chopped tomato

1 cup coarsely chopped onion

1/4 pound fresh okra, ends trimmed

1 fresh green chili (serrano or Thai),
  split lengthwise

1/4 cup cilantro leaves

3 teaspoons Sambar Powder
  (page 222)

1 1/2 teaspoons salt

1/4 teaspoon mustard seeds

1 dried red chili

10 to 15 fresh curry leaves

1/2 teaspoon fresh lemon juice

Sambar is a full-bodied South Indian dhal and vegetable preparation seasoned with asafetida and fenugreek. It is a mainstay among vegetarians, as it is flavorful and rich in protein. It can be eaten with rice (in place of dhal) or as an accompaniment to Sourdough Crepes (page 40), Sourdough Crepes with Vegetables (page 44), or Sourdough Dumplings (page 46) for a first course.

1. In a bowl rinse the dhal in cold water until the water is no longer cloudy. Combine the washed dhal, 1 1/4 cups water, and turmeric in a small saucepan and bring to a boil. Reduce the heat to low, cover, and cook for 30 minutes (45 minutes for yellow split peas), until the peas are soft.

2. Combine the tamarind concentrate with 2 tablespoons hot water and break it up with your fingers to dissolve it completely.

3. In a 3- or 4-quart saucepan, heat 1 tablespoon of the oil over medium-high heat. Add the fenugreek seeds and asafetida, and when the fenugreek seeds start to brown add 2 cups water, the potato, tomato, onion, okra, green chili, cilantro, sambar powder, salt, and dissolved tamarind. Bring the mixture to a boil, reduce the heat, and simmer 20 minutes or until the potatoes are tender.

4. When the dhal is cooked, mash it up with a potato masher to break up the peas. Stir this into the cooked vegetables and simmer together for another 10 minutes. The mixture should be

the consistency of thin pea soup (thinner than dhal). Remove from the heat.

5. In a small frying pan heat the remaining 1 tablespoon oil over medium-high heat. Add the mustard seeds and cover. When the mustard seeds have popped, toss in the dried red chili and curry leaves. After the leaves crackle for a few seconds, pour the contents into the vegetable and dhal mixture.

6. Add the lemon juice and taste for salt.

PREPARATION TIME: 45 MINUTES

SERVES: 6

RECIPE MAY BE PREPARED IN ADVANCE AND REHEATED.

Spicy Dhal and Shallot Stew
(Onion *Sambar*)

¹/₂ cup thoor dhal or yellow split peas

¹/₈ teaspoon turmeric

¹/₄ cup grated unsweetened coconut

¹/₄ teaspoon tamarind concentrate

6 teaspoons Sambar Powder
  (page 222)

1 teaspoon garbanzo flour (*besan*,
  gram flour) (optional)

10 fresh curry leaves

1 cup peeled, quartered shallots

1 fresh green chili (serrano or Thai),
  split lengthwise

1 to 1¹/₄ teaspoons salt

1 tablespoon vegetable oil

¹/₄ teaspoon mustard seeds

¹/₄ teaspoon fenugreek seeds

2 dried red chilies

My aunt makes my favorite version of *sambar* with tiny purple onions and toasted coconut. I substitute shallots, which are quite delicious in this recipe. It makes an excellent vegetarian meal served with rice, Eggplant in Tamarind Sauce (page 70), Green Beans with Urad Dhal (page 73), and Tomato and Cucumber with Mustard Seeds (page 85).

1. In a bowl rinse the dhal in cold water until the water is no longer cloudy. Bring the dhal, 1¹/₄ cups water, and turmeric to a boil in a 2-quart saucepan. Lower the heat and simmer, partly covered, for 30 minutes (45 minutes for yellow split peas) until the dhal is tender. Thoroughly mash the dhal with a potato masher or the back of a spoon.

2. Toast the coconut in a dry frying pan over medium heat, stirring constantly until it turns cinnamon brown and no white remains. Place the toasted coconut in a dry blender or food processor and process to a fine powder. Set aside.

3. Dissolve the tamarind concentrate in 2 tablespoons hot water, breaking up the lumps completely with your fingers.

4. When the dhal has finished cooking, add the toasted coconut, dissolved tamarind, sambar powder, garbanzo flour, curry leaves, shallots, green chili, salt, and 1¹/₄ cups water. Simmer 15 minutes or until the shallots are tender. Add more water if the mixture gets very thick. It should be the consistency of thin pea soup (thinner than dhal).

5. In a small frying pan heat the oil over medium-high heat.

Add the mustard seeds and cover. After the seeds have popped for a few seconds, put in the fenugreek seeds and red chilies. When the fenugreek seeds and chilies have browned pour the mixture into the dhal and stir.

PREPARATION TIME: 1 HOUR
SERVES: 6
RECIPE MAY BE PREPARED IN ADVANCE AND REHEATED.

Stringing up dried red chilies in Adur.

Dhal and Pepper Broth
(Pepper *Rasam*)

1 cup thoor dhal or yellow split peas

1/8 teaspoon turmeric

1 tablespoon tamarind pulp

3 tablespoons vegetable oil

1 1/2 teaspoons mustard seeds

1 teaspoon cumin seeds

1 teaspoon black peppercorns, crushed with a mortar and pestle or coffee grinder

1/4 teaspoon fenugreek seeds

20 fresh curry leaves

2 dried red chilies

1/4 teaspoon ground asafetida

1 cup chopped tomato

1 cup sliced onion

1 1/2 teaspoons salt

2 to 3 teaspoons fresh lemon juice (depending on the sourness of the tomato)

This pungent broth, called "pepper water" by the British, is usually served in stainless steel tumblers and either drunk or poured over rice. It's considered a healing drink for people with colds because the pepper clears the sinuses. I serve it as a light first course with an Indian meal.

1. Wash the thoor dhal in a bowl with several changes of cold water. When the water runs clear, drain completely. Place the dhal, 2 1/2 cups water, and turmeric in a heavy 3- or 4-quart stockpot and bring to a boil. Reduce the heat, cover, and simmer 30 minutes (45 minutes for yellow split peas) until the water has been absorbed and the peas break under pressure from the back of a spoon. When the dhal is cooked, mash it *thoroughly* with a potato masher or the back of a spoon to a pastelike consistency.

2. Soak the tamarind in 1 cup hot water. Break up the lumps with your hands and set aside for 10 minutes. Strain and discard the solids. Set the liquid aside.

3. Heat the oil in a frying pan. Add the mustard seeds and cover. When the seeds pop, put in the cumin seeds, peppercorns, and fenugreek seeds and fry briefly until the cumin seeds brown. Toss in the curry leaves, dried red chilies, and asafetida. After the curry leaves crackle for a few seconds add the entire mixture to the dhal.

4. Stir in the tomato, onion, salt, and tamarind juice, and 3 cups

water, and bring to a boil. Reduce the heat and simmer, partly covered, for 30 minutes.
5. Add the lemon juice and remove from the heat. Taste to make sure it is slightly sour and adjust lemon juice accordingly. To serve: stir the broth but allow the lentil solids to settle for a few seconds before spooning it into bowls. The broth should appear cloudy with bits of vegetable and seeds floating in it.

PREPARATION TIME: 1 HOUR 10 MINUTES
SERVES: 6 TO 8
RECIPE MAY BE PREPARED IN ADVANCE AND REHEATED.

Fish and Seafood

With 360 miles of coastline and over 1,000 miles of inland waterways, Kerala is well supplied with salt and fresh-water fish. The industry is visible everywhere: beaches near Kovalam are filled with colorful fishing boats, large insectlike Chinese fishing nets dot the shore near the port of Kochi, and small boats with patchwork sails push off into Vembanad Lake at dusk. A fishmonger comes to my aunt's kitchen door a few times a week and cleans the fish she picks from the basket.

Some people prefer the milder taste of local fresh-water fish such as pearl spot and freshwater grouper, and consider them ideal for wrapping in banana leaves and cooking on a slow fire. But others enjoy flavorful saltwater varieties like pomfret (a flat bony fish with dense white flesh), Spanish mackerel (a rich oily fish), and Indian salmon (less rich than true salmon). Bony fish are rubbed with masala and fried, and fleshy fish

Freshly caught anchovies will go into curries and pickles.

are cut up and cooked in a curry, or stuffed with a spicy masala.

People in Kerala prefer to cook their fish in an earthenware *chutty* (thick pot), regardless of whether they are simmering it in liquid or roasting it between banana leaves. They insist the flavor is superior to that of fish cooked in a metal vessel. They also never stir fish curries that have sauces because it would break apart the pieces. Instead, they pick up the pot and swirl the sauce in the pan a few times during the cooking, to circulate the heat and the liquid.

The way in which cooks flavor their fish curries may vary according to the part of the state they are from. In central Kerala, with its many Syrian Christians, people use the extremely sour dried fruit called *kodumpuli* (*gamboge* or fish tamarind) because it gets rid of the "fishy" flavor as well as providing enough citric acid to act as a preservative. Some cooks choose to use the sour juice of the tamarind fruit, and in the northern part of the state they cut up small green mangoes to make their fish curries tart.

Shellfish are eaten by those who live near the coast, but rarely by people inland. What Indians call "shrimp" are tiny versions of what we buy, and because of their size, the flavors of the masala can permeate them fully. In some cases, I suggest cutting large shrimp into smaller pieces so the flavors can be similarly absorbed. "Prawns" in India are closer to our jumbo-size shrimp, and are good for *biriyani* (a flavorful rice casserole). The mussels and clams collected off the coast are particularly good steamed in coconut milk and spices, or stuffed with rice paste and deep-fried.

All fish and seafood curries should be prepared just before serving. If they are left to sit they turn watery and flat-tasting, and they cannot be rewarmed without becoming overcooked. Since the pieces can be delicate, I transfer the fish to a serving bowl first, then pour the sauce over the top.

Fish with Sour Mango

Fish in Fragrant Coconut Milk (*Meen Molee*)

Stuffed Fish with Sweet and Spicy Masala

Fish with Red Sauce (*Meen Vevichathu*)

Fish with Cilantro and Coconut

Baked Fish with Tamarind (*Meen Chuttathu*)

Stir-Fried Shrimp with Coconut (*Chemeen Thoren*)

Tamarind Shrimp (Prawns *Varathiathu*)

Shrimp in Coconut Milk (*Chemeen Pappas*)

Shrimp with Cracked Pepper and Curry Leaves

Steamed Mussels in Coconut Milk

(See Rice and Breads chapter for Fish *Biriyani* and Shrimp *Biriyani*)

Fish with Sour Mango

1 green mango (preferably small)
1 cup grated unsweetened coconut
$^1/_2$ cup finely chopped onion
20 fresh curry leaves
Ground masala
  • 1 teaspoon coriander
  • $^1/_2$ teaspoon cayenne
  • $^1/_4$ teaspoon turmeric
1 teaspoon salt
1$^1/_2$ pounds 1-inch-thick swordfish steaks, skinned and cut into 1-inch cubes
1 to 2 fresh green chilies (serrano or Thai), according to taste, very thinly sliced
1 tablespoon coconut oil (optional)

My aunt makes this exquisite curry by poaching small fish steaks (I use swordfish) in a grated coconut sauce flavored with unripe green mango, curry leaves, and green chilies. Green mango adds a sour element that's complex and fruity: try to use the small variety sold at Indian groceries because they are more sour than the large ones. If using the large type, make a batch of Hot Mango Pickle (page 192) with the unused fruit.

1. Cut the mango (with the skin) into irregular slices approximately 1 x 1 inch and $^1/_2$ inch thick. Measure 1 cup and set aside.

2. In a blender combine the coconut, onion, 8 of the curry leaves, and the ground masala. Process on high speed, adding $^3/_4$ cup water (or more) to form a thick paste like pesto.

3. In a wide deep pan combine the coconut paste, 1 cup water, and salt. Add the fish and gently bring to a boil. Add the mango pieces, sliced chilies, and the remaining 12 curry leaves. Simmer on medium-low heat, uncovered, for about 10 minutes, until the fish is just cooked and the mango begins to turn translucent. Do not overcook. There will be a lot of thick sauce.

4. Drizzle the coconut oil over the top and remove from the heat. Serve immediately.

PREPARATION TIME: 30 MINUTES
SERVES: 6
RECIPE MAY BE PREPARED IN ADVANCE THROUGH STEP 2.

Preparing Fish with Sour Mango in an earthenware pot.
Aunty gently swirls the pan to keep the fish intact.

Fish in Fragrant Coconut Milk
(*Meen Molee*)

4 tablespoons vegetable oil

2 cups thinly sliced onions

2 medium garlic cloves, thinly sliced

6 thin slices ginger

1 fresh green chili (serrano or Thai),
   split lengthwise

10 to 12 fresh curry leaves

Ground masala
- 1 teaspoon coriander
- $^1/_4$ teaspoon cumin
- $^1/_4$ teaspoon turmeric
- $^1/_4$ teaspoon black pepper

1 cup chopped tomato, plus a few
   thinly sliced cross sections for
   garnish

1 teaspoon salt

$1^1/_2$ pounds skinned white fish fillets
   (cod or haddock), cut into
   2-inch pieces

$^1/_2$ cup canned coconut milk

Molee is one of the best-known fish curries in Kerala and the Syrian Christians and Hindus are especially fond of it. This recipe comes from a Syrian Christian friend, Nimmy Paul. It has a mild coconut sauce with a touch of tartness, and a sliced tomato garnish.

1. In a 12-inch frying pan with a lid heat the oil. Fry the onions, garlic, ginger, green chili, and curry leaves until the onions are lightly browned. Add the ground masala, tomato, and salt and fry 10 to 15 minutes, until the tomato becomes soft and begins to break down.

2. Push the mixture to the sides of the pan and place the fish pieces in a single layer in the center. With a spatula, smear the paste over the fish. Combine the coconut milk with $^1/_2$ cup water, and pour it over the fish. Gently shake the pan to circulate the liquid without disturbing the fish. Cover and cook at a low simmer for 10 minutes or more, depending on the thickness of the fish. It is not necessary to turn the fish, but if you do, take care to ensure that the pieces do not break apart. The sauce will be fairly thin. Check the salt.

3. Carefully transfer the fish pieces to a low serving bowl; pour the sauce over them. Garnish with the tomato slices and serve.

PREPARATION TIME: 40 MINUTES

SERVES: 6

RECIPE MAY BE PREPARED AHEAD OF TIME THROUGH STEP 1.

Stuffed Fish with Sweet and Spicy Masala

Marinade

1 (2- to 3-pound) whole bluefish, cleaned

1/4 teaspoon cayenne

1/4 teaspoon turmeric

1/4 teaspoon salt

Garnish

1 teaspoon Ghee (page 218) or butter

2 tablespoons broken cashews

2 tablespoons golden raisins

Masala

1/3 cup vegetable oil

4 cups sliced onions

1 tablespoon minced garlic

1 tablespoon minced ginger

2 fresh green chilies, split lengthwise

1/4 cup chopped fresh cilantro

1/4 cup chopped fresh mint leaves

Ground masala

- 4 teaspoons coriander
- 1 teaspoon cumin
- 1/2 teaspoon cayenne
- 1/2 teaspoon turmeric

1/2 teaspoon Garam Masala (page 223)

1 cup chopped tomato

1 teaspoon fresh lime juice

1 teaspoon salt

1/2 teaspoon sugar

This is an outstanding fish recipe from Mrs. V. C. Faiza, a Muslim cooking instructor from northern Kerala. Sweet caramelized onions plus hot cayenne pepper make this a wonderfully robust dish. Faiza used pomfret, a rather flat, dense, white-fleshed fish, but bluefish is easier to find here, and I love its buttery texture for this dish.

1. Remove the head and tail from the fish. Butterfly it by slicing down the entire length of the belly side. Open it up and carefully remove the backbone, starting from the neck. Remove any remaining bones. Fold the fish in half, skin side out, and rub the skin with a mixture of the cayenne, turmeric, and salt. Marinate for 15 minutes.

2. In a frying pan, heat the ghee (or butter) over medium heat. Fry the cashews until golden. Remove to a plate. In the remaining ghee fry the raisins until they swell and brown slightly. Add them to the cashews and set aside.

3. In a 12-inch nonstick frying pan heat the oil and fry the onions until the edges are nicely browned. Add the garlic, ginger, green chilies, cilantro, and mint, and stir for 1 minute.

Stir in the ground masala, garam masala, tomato, lime juice, salt, and sugar, and fry until the onions are well browned, and the mixture is thick and pastelike. Remove from the heat and cool slightly.

4. Open the fish and spread one quarter to one third of the onion mixture inside; fold it over to close. In the same frying pan push the remaining onion mixture to the sides of the pan and place the fish in the middle. Turn the heat to medium and when the onion mixture simmers turn to low and cover. Cook for 10 minutes, until the bottom of the fish is lightly browned, and carefully turn over. Cover and continue cooking another 10 minutes to brown the other side. Remove from the heat.

5. Carefully transfer the fish to a platter. Spread the remaining sauce over the fish and garnish it with the cashews and raisins; serve immediately.

PREPARATION TIME: 1¹/₂ HOURS
SERVES: 6 TO 8
RECIPE MAY BE PREPARED IN ADVANCE THROUGH STEP 3.

Cantilevered "Chinese" fishing nets line the shores of Kochi Harbor, more for show now than for use.

Fishermen haul in their catch at Adimalathura Beach.

Fish with Red Sauce
(*Meen Vevichathu*)

2 tablespoons vegetable oil
1½ cups thinly sliced onions
1½ teaspoons minced garlic
1½ teaspoons minced ginger
10 to 12 fresh curry leaves
Ground masala
  • 3 teaspoons coriander
  • ¾ teaspoon cayenne
  • ¼ teaspoon turmeric
¼ teaspoon fenugreek seeds, finely
  ground in a coffee grinder or mini
  food processor
1½ cups chopped tomato
1½ teaspoons salt
1½ pounds skinned white fish fillets
  (cod or haddock), cut into
  2-inch pieces
1 tablespoon coconut oil (optional)

This curry is a classic part of a Syrian Christian wedding feast. It is often made with the sour fruit called *kodumpuli,* which turns it a deep red color. Since the fruit is so high in citric acid it acts as a preservative, allowing the wedding chefs to start cooking fish curry for 1,000 people days before the event. My version uses tomato to get the red color and the sour flavor.

1. In a wide nonstick pan (large enough to hold the fish in a single layer) heat the vegetable oil over medium-high heat. Add the onions and sauté until the edges just begin to brown. Add the garlic, ginger, and curry leaves and fry for 1 minute. Stir in the ground masala and fenugreek and fry briefly. Now put in the tomato and salt and continue frying until the tomatoes break down and form a paste.

2. Add ½ cup water and bring to a boil. Place the fish pieces in the pan without stacking them, and spoon the sauce over them. Bring to a boil, reduce the heat to low, and simmer, covered, for about 10 minutes or until the fish is flaky in the thickest part. Drizzle with the coconut oil, carefully transfer to a serving dish, and serve immediately.

PREPARATION TIME: 35 MINUTES
SERVES: 6
RECIPE MAY BE PREPARED IN ADVANCE THROUGH STEP 1.

Fish with Cilantro and Coconut

3/4 cup grated unsweetened coconut

1/2 cup loosely packed fresh cilantro leaves, plus 2 tablespoons coarsely chopped leaves for garnish

Ground masala

- 2 teaspoons cumin
- 1/4 teaspoon cayenne
- 1/4 teaspoon turmeric

3 tablespoons vegetable oil

1 1/2 cups thinly sliced onions

2 teaspoons minced garlic

2 fresh green chilies (serrano or Thai), split lengthwise

1 teaspoon salt

1 1/2 pounds skinned fish fillets (cod or haddock), cut into 2-inch pieces

PREPARATION TIME: 35 MINUTES
SERVES: 6
RECIPE MAY BE PREPARED IN ADVANCE THROUGH STEP 2.

Many of the Jews who settled in Kochi came from Iraq, and this is a curry from that community. It includes plenty of Kerala's coconut and is flavored with fresh cilantro and dried cumin—both commonly used ingredients in Iraqi Jewish cooking. Serve this dish with Chickpeas with Onion (page 78), Thoor Dhal with Tomato and Onion (page 106), and plain rice.

1. In a blender or food processor, blend the coconut, 1/2 cup cilantro, ground masala, and 3/4 cup water (or more) together to form a paste like thick pesto. Set aside.

2. Heat the oil in a 12-inch nonstick frying pan over medium-high heat. Add the onions and fry until the edges begin to brown. Add the garlic and green chilies and fry another minute. Stir in the coconut paste, 3/4 cup water, and salt and bring to a boil. Reduce the heat and simmer 8 to 10 minutes, until the mixture thickens and turns a little darker. If it dries out, add more water.

3. Stir in another 1/2 cup water. Place the fish pieces in the pan and spoon the sauce over them. When the mixture returns to a boil, reduce the heat to low and simmer, partly covered, for 8 to 12 minutes (depending on the thickness of the fish) until the fish is flaky and just opaque in the thickest part. Do not turn the pieces, but occasionally swirl the pan to circulate the sauce. Remove from the heat and taste for salt.

4. Carefully transfer the fish pieces to a low serving bowl. Pour the sauce over the fish and garnish with the chopped cilantro.

Baked Fish with Tamarind
(*Meen Chuttathu*)

8 to 10 dried red chilies

1 (1-inch) ball tamarind pulp

2 tablespoons coconut oil or
vegetable oil

1 cup finely chopped shallots

1 1/2 teaspoons minced garlic

2 teaspoons minced ginger

1/2 teaspoon fennel seeds, ground
with a mortar and pestle

3/4 teaspoon salt

1/2 cup seeded chopped tomato

1 1/2 pounds skinned white fish fillets
(cod or haddock), cut into 2-inch
pieces

1 tablespoon coconut oil (optional)

SOAKING TIME: 2 HOURS
PREPARATION TIME: 45 MINUTES
SERVES: 6
RECIPE MAY BE PREPARED IN
ADVANCE THROUGH STEP 3.

Traditionally this dish is made by placing fish between banana leaves and roasting it in a dry earthenware pot. When the banana leaf chars on the bottom of the pot, it gives the dish a smoky flavor.

1. Snap the chilies in half and discard the seeds. Bring the skins and 1 cup water to a boil in a small saucepan. Cover (remove from the heat, and set aside) for 2 hours. Drain the chilies and process to a fine paste in a mini food processor.

2. In a small bowl combine the tamarind pulp and 1/2 cup hot water. Using your fingers, thoroughly break up the tamarind. Set aside for 5 minutes, then strain the liquid into another container and discard the solids.

3. In a nonstick pan heat the oil over medium heat. Add the shallots and fry until the edges turn brown. Add the chili paste, garlic, ginger, fennel, and salt. Fry until the seasonings give off their aroma. Stir in the tomato and tamarind juice and continue frying until the tomato softens.

4. Preheat the oven to 375 degrees F. Place a large piece of parchment paper or aluminum foil on a cookie sheet. Put the fillets, skin side down, in the middle of it. Spread the chili mixture evenly on top of the fish pieces. Sprinkle the coconut oil over the fish, and fold the edges of the parchment or foil to seal tightly. Bake 15 minutes or more depending on the thickness of the fillet. Remove the parchment or foil and transfer the fish to a serving platter. Serve immediately.

Stir-Fried Shrimp with Coconut
(*Chemeen Thoren*)

$^3/_4$ cup grated unsweetened coconut

2 garlic cloves, crushed

1 fresh green chili (serrano or Thai),
  split lengthwise

$^3/_4$ to 1 teaspoon salt

Ground masala

  • 1 teaspoon coriander

  • $^1/_4$ teaspoon cayenne

  • $^1/_4$ teaspoon turmeric

3 tablespoons vegetable oil

1 teaspoon mustard seeds

2 dried red chilies

10 fresh curry leaves

$1^1/_2$ pounds shrimp (any size), shelled
  and deveined, cut into $^1/_4$-inch
  pieces

The grated coconut stir-fry known as *thoren* is made here with chopped shrimp. It's a fast, easy, and very tasty dish.

1. Combine the coconut, garlic, green chili, salt, and ground masala in a bowl with about $^1/_4$ cup water to make a moist ball. Set aside.

2. In a wok heat the oil over medium-high heat. Add the mustard seeds and cover. When the seeds have popped, toss in the red chilies and curry leaves. After the leaves crackle for a few seconds, put in the shrimp and stir-fry for 1 minute. Stir in the coconut mixture and continue frying for another 3 minutes or until the shrimp are just cooked through.

PREPARATION TIME: 25 MINUTES

SERVES: 6

RECIPE MAY BE PREPARED IN ADVANCE THROUGH STEP 1.

Tamarind Shrimp
(Prawns *Varathiathu*)

1 1/2 pounds medium or large shrimp, peeled and deveined

1/4 teaspoon cayenne

1/4 teaspoon turmeric

1 1/4 teaspoons salt

5 tablespoons vegetable oil

1/2 teaspoon tamarind concentrate

1/2 teaspoon mustard seeds

1/8 teaspoon fenugreek seeds

10 to 12 fresh curry leaves

2 cups thinly sliced onions

1 1/2 teaspoons minced garlic

1 1/2 teaspoons minced ginger

1 teaspoon minced fresh green chili (serrano or Thai)

3/4 cup chopped tomato

Ground masala
- 3 teaspoons coriander
- 3/4 teaspoon cayenne
- 1/2 teaspoon cumin

This outstanding Mappila curry from Mrs. V. C. Faiza has a thick tangy tamarind and red chili sauce.

1. Rub the shrimp with a mixture of cayenne, turmeric, and 1/4 teaspoon of the salt. Marinate for 15 minutes.
2. Heat 2 tablespoons of the oil over medium-high heat, and fry the shrimp briefly until they begin to turn pink (2 to 3 minutes). Do not cook all the way through. Set aside.
3. Soak the tamarind in 1/4 cup hot water, breaking it up with your fingers until dissolved. Set aside.
4. Heat the remaining 3 tablespoons oil in a wide deep frying pan over medium-high heat. Add the mustard seeds and cover. When the mustard seeds pop, add the fenugreek seeds and as soon as they brown, put in the curry leaves; after they crackle for a few seconds, add the onions. Fry until the edges of the onions begin to brown. Stir in the garlic, ginger, and green chili. When the onions are very brown, add the dissolved tamarind, tomato, ground masala, and the remaining 1 teaspoon salt. Stir constantly until the tomato breaks down. If it dries out, sprinkle in a little more water—the sauce should be very thick. Add the shrimp and stir until they are just cooked through (about 5 minutes).

PREPARATION TIME: 45 MINUTES
SERVES: 6
RECIPE MAY BE PREPARED IN ADVANCE THROUGH STEP 3.

Shrimp in Coconut Milk
(*Chemeen Pappas*)

3 tablespoons vegetable oil

1 teaspoon mustard seeds

$1/8$ teaspoon fenugreek seeds

10 fresh curry leaves

2 cups thinly sliced onions

2 teaspoons minced garlic

1 teaspoon minced ginger

2 fresh green chilies (serrano or Thai),
    split lengthwise

2 teaspoons tomato paste

Ground masala
  - 4 teaspoons coriander
  - $1/2$ teaspoon paprika
  - $1/4$ teaspoon cayenne
  - $1/4$ teaspoon black pepper

$1 1/4$ teaspoons salt

$3/4$ cup canned coconut milk

$1 1/2$ pounds medium or large shrimp,
    peeled and deveined, sliced in half
    lengthwise if large

This classic Kerala curry is typically made with very small shrimp, which means the flavors of the sauce mingle well with the shellfish. I use the smallest shrimp I can buy, or I cut larger shrimp in half lengthwise (this makes them curl nicely). The sauce should have a pinkish color; do not fry the onions too much or the sauce will turn dark.

1. In a large nonstick pan heat the oil over medium-high heat. Add the mustard seeds and cover. When the seeds have popped, add the fenugreek seeds and fry until slightly browned. Add the curry leaves and after they crackle for a few seconds, put in the onions and fry until soft. Stir in the garlic, ginger, and green chilies and fry for 1 minute. Add the tomato paste, ground masala, and salt and fry for another minute. If the mixture dries out, sprinkle in a little water. Add $1/2$ cup of the coconut milk and 1 cup water. Bring the mixture to a boil, reduce the heat, and simmer, uncovered, over medium-high heat for 5 to 10 minutes to blend the flavors and thicken the sauce.

2. Put in the shrimp and stir constantly for 4 to 6 minutes or until the shrimp are opaque and cooked through. Add the remaining $1/4$ cup of coconut milk, bring just to a boil, and remove from the heat. Taste for salt and serve immediately.

PREPARATION TIME: 40 MINUTES

SERVES: 6

RECIPE MAY BE PREPARED IN ADVANCE THROUGH STEP 1.

Shrimp with Cracked Pepper and Curry Leaves

3 tablespoons coconut oil (no substitutions)

1 1/2 teaspoons black peppercorns, well crushed with a mortar and pestle (no large pieces)

1 1/2 pounds medium shrimp (not jumbo), peeled and deveined, leaving the last segment and the tail attached

30 fresh curry leaves

3/4 teaspoon salt

This stir-fry was inspired by a dish I tasted at the Mumbai restaurant Only Fish. It brings together the simple intensity of pepper, curry leaves, and coconut oil—three quintessentially Keralan ingredients. It also happens to be a very pretty dish, especially if the tails are left on the shrimp. Use medium shrimp so the flavors can penetrate.

In a wok heat the coconut oil over medium-high heat. (*Note:* coconut oil has a low smoking point, so do not let it get too hot.) Add the crushed peppercorns and stir for 1 minute until the peppercorns release their aroma. Put in the shrimp and stir-fry until they just lose their translucent quality and turn pink. Toss in the curry leaves and salt and continue stirring over the heat 1 to 2 minutes until the shrimp are opaque and the curry leaves give off their fragrance. (There is no sauce but the shrimp will be glossy and flecked with peppercorns and curry leaves.) Serve immediately.

PREPARATION TIME: 25 MINUTES
SERVES: 6
RECIPE SHOULD BE COOKED JUST PRIOR TO SERVING.

Steamed Mussels in Coconut Milk

4 tablespoons vegetable oil
2 cups thinly sliced onions
1 tablespoon minced ginger
Ground masala
- 3 teaspoons coriander
- $1/2$ teaspoon turmeric
- $1/2$ teaspoon cayenne

$3/4$ teaspoon salt
2 cups canned coconut milk
3 pounds fresh mussels, or small
    clams, scrubbed and debearded
1 tablespoon fresh lemon juice
$1/4$ cup chopped cilantro

Mussels and clams are harvested along the coast of Kerala, and they are very tasty steamed in coconut milk. This recipe is extremely simple, yet it has vibrant tropical flavors that make it a real winner. It makes a great first course served in shallow bowls with lots of sauce.

1. Heat the oil in a large Dutch oven. Add the onions and fry over medium-high heat until the edges turn light brown. Next add the ginger and continue frying for 1 minute, stirring constantly. Put in the ground masala and stir for another 1 to 2 minutes.

2. Add the salt, coconut milk, and 1 cup water and bring to a boil. Now put in the mussels, spooning some of the sauce over them. Cover and steam 7 minutes or until all the shells open. Remove from the heat. Discard any shells that aren't open.

3. Sprinkle with the lemon juice and cilantro and stir gently. Spoon the mussels into individual bowls along with some of the sauce. Serve immediately.

PREPARATION TIME: 35 MINUTES
SERVES: 8 AS A FIRST COURSE
RECIPE MAY BE PREPARED IN ADVANCE THROUGH STEP 1.

Chicken, Eggs, and Meat

Syrian Christians and Mappilas (Kerala Muslims) are renowned for their rich and robust meat preparations. The big feasts associated with Christmas, Easter, Id, and Ramadan (after fasting), give these groups an opportunity to feast on such specialties as Syrian Christian meat stews, poultry roasts, and "meat fries"; and Muslim chicken kurmas, and beef and liver curries. The use of coconut, curry leaves, crushed peppercorns, and cashews gives these dishes a uniquely tropical twist, quite distinct from the meat curries of North India.

Kerala is one of the few states in India where the slaughter of beef is legal. Although it is taboo for Hindus to consume it, beef is often eaten by Christians and Muslims. They also eat goat, lamb, poultry, and eggs, as do some Hindus in Kerala. The Jews of Kochi had facilities for slaughtering chickens according to their religious laws, so chicken was often eaten on the Sabbath, since

When browned in oil, whole dried red chilies lend a subtle heat to South Indian curries.

fish was considered too ordinary for that day and beef was avoided out of respect for Hindus.

Chicken curries are made with a whole bird cut into small pieces, bone in. The bones make the curry very tasty, but also a little more trouble to eat. To make it easier, use boneless skinless chicken thighs and breasts, or if you prefer to use chicken on the bone, increase the amount from two pounds boneless meat to three pounds of meat with bone.

Eggs are not eaten as often as poultry or meat in Kerala, but they are prepared in some very delicious ways using coconut and curry leaves. I was raised on spicy egg curries and I encourage non-Indians to discover how exciting they can be.

Red meat in India is not as tender and fleshy as here, so such techniques as boiling meat in water with spices, or cooking with vinegar, help tenderize it. Another method is to stir-fry the meat for a long time in a little liquid. Cooks in Kerala believe that the more you fry meat, the tastier and more succulent it becomes, and in developing these recipes I too found that vigorous frying for the last 5 to 10 minutes helps make the meat softer. Many of the techniques for cooking meat in Kerala go against Western practices. The results, though, prove there is more than one path to perfection.

Fragrant Chicken Stir-Fry (Chicken *Piralen*)

Chicken with Potato and Fennel Seeds
(Chicken with *Pacha Masala*)

Chicken with Toasted Masala (Chicken *Varutharacha*)

Peppery Chicken Curry

Coriander Chicken (*Malli Char*)

Chicken *Kurma*

Chicken with Green Chilies and Tamarind
(Chili Chicken)

Eggs with Spicy Masala (Egg Roast)

Eggs Stirred with Coconut (Egg *Thoren*)

Minced Beef with Coconut (Meat *Thoren*)

Spicy Beef Curry

Beef in Fragrant Coconut Milk (Meat Stew)

Spicy Chicken Liver Curry (Liver Fry)

Peppery Stir-Fried Lamb (Meat Fry)

Lamb *Vindaloo*

(See Rice and Breads chapter for Lamb *Biriyani*)

Fragrant Chicken Stir-Fry
(Chicken *Piralen*)

2 pounds boneless skinless chicken thighs and breasts, trimmed and cut into 1-inch cubes

Ground masala
- 5 teaspoons coriander
- 1 teaspoon cumin
- $1/2$ teaspoon cayenne
- $1/4$ teaspoon turmeric
- $1/8$ teaspoon cinnamon
- $1/8$ teaspoon clove

$1/2$ teaspoon black peppercorns, coarsely ground with a mortar and pestle

$1/2$ teaspoon fennel seeds, finely ground with a mortar and pestle

4 teaspoons white vinegar

4 tablespoons vegetable oil

1 cup sliced onion

2 teaspoons minced garlic

2 teaspoons minced ginger

1 teaspoon salt

$1/2$ teaspoon mustard seeds

10 to 12 fresh curry leaves

$1/2$ cup thinly sliced shallots or onion

Piralen is a dish I learned from Syrian Christian cooks in Kerala. It is a technique in which the meat juices and spices create a creamy coating that clings to the meat. It makes for a moist and flavorful stir-fry.

1. Marinate the chicken in a mixture of the ground masala, black pepper, fennel, and vinegar for 1 hour.

2. In a large nonstick frying pan heat 3 tablespoons of the oil over medium-high heat. Fry the onions until the edges begin to brown. Stir in the garlic and ginger and continue frying for 1 minute. Add the marinated chicken and stir constantly until all the pink color disappears. Sprinkle in the salt and continue frying until the chicken is cooked through and there is just enough sauce to coat the pieces. Remove from the heat and taste for salt. Place the chicken on a serving dish.

3. In a small frying pan, heat the remaining 1 tablespoon of oil over medium-high heat. Add the mustard seeds and cover. When the seeds have popped, toss in the curry leaves and let them crackle for a few seconds. Put in the shallots and continue frying until well browned. Pour the mixture over the chicken and serve immediately.

MARINATING TIME: 1 HOUR
PREPARATION TIME: 30 MINUTES
SERVES: 6 TO 8
RECIPE MAY BE PREPARED IN ADVANCE THROUGH STEP 1.

Chicken with Potato and Fennel Seeds
(Chicken with *Pacha Masala*)

2 small boiling potatoes, peeled and
cut into 1-inch cubes

2 pounds boneless skinless chicken
thighs, trimmed and cut into 1-inch
pieces

$3/4$ teaspoon turmeric

5 tablespoons vegetable oil

2 cups thinly sliced onion plus
$1/2$ cup coarsely chopped onion

$1^1/2$ tablespoons chopped garlic

2 tablespoons chopped ginger

1 to 2 fresh green chilies (serrano or
Thai), coarsely chopped

Ground masala

- 6 teaspoons coriander
- 1 teaspoon cumin
- $1/2$ teaspoon cayenne
- $1/8$ teaspoon cinnamon
- $1/8$ teaspoon clove

1 teaspoon fennel seeds, coarsely
ground with a mortar and pestle

1 cup chopped tomatoes

$1^1/4$ to $1^1/2$ teaspoons salt

The phrase *pacha masala* means "fresh mixture" in Malayalam, and it refers to the blend of crushed raw onion, garlic, ginger, and green chili, that thickens and flavors this curry. It has a dark, deeply flavored sauce and it tastes even better the next day. My cousin Padma has perfected this dish, and this is her recipe.

1. Parboil the potatoes in salted water for 5 to 7 minutes. Drain.
2. Sprinkle the chicken with turmeric and coat completely. Heat 1 tablespoon of the oil in a large deep nonstick pan or Dutch oven and add the chicken pieces, stirring constantly over high heat for about 5 minutes or until it loses its pink color. Transfer the chicken and juices to a bowl.
3. In the same pan, wiped clean, heat the remaining 4 teaspoons oil over medium-high heat. Fry the sliced onion until the edges turn brown. Remove the fried onion to a plate, leaving behind any oil in the pan.
4. In a food processor combine chopped onion, garlic, ginger, and green chili and process to a medium-fine consistency, so the largest pieces of onion are only $1/4$ inch big. Be sure not to liquify the onion or it will not brown in the next step.
5. Put the chopped onion mixture in the frying pan over medium-high heat and stir constantly until the mixture turns light brown. Add another tablespoon of oil, if needed, to prevent sticking.
6. Stir in the previously browned onions, ground masala, fennel, tomatoes, and salt and fry for 2 minutes until the

tomatoes become soft and begin to break up. Add $^1/_4$ cup water and stir until tomatoes break down and mixture forms a paste.

7. Add the chicken and its juices, the parboiled potatoes, and another $^1/_4$ cup water and bring to a boil. Reduce the heat to low, and simmer, covered, for 30 minutes, stirring occasionally. The sauce should be dark and relatively thick. Add more water if too dry, or remove cover to thicken sauce if too watery. Taste for salt.

PREPARATION TIME: 1 HOUR 15 MINUTES
SERVES: 6
RECIPE MAY BE PREPARED A DAY IN ADVANCE AND REHEATED.

Chicken with Toasted Masala
(Chicken *Varutharacha*)

3/4 cup grated unsweetened coconut

4 teaspoons ground coriander

1/4 teaspoon cayenne

4 tablespoons vegetable oil

2 cups thinly sliced onion

2 teaspoons minced garlic

2 teaspoons minced ginger

1 fresh green chili (serrano or Thai), split lengthwise

10 fresh curry leaves

1 dried red chili

Ground masala
- 1/4 teaspoon turmeric
- 1/8 teaspoon black pepper
- 1/8 teaspoon cinnamon
- 1/8 teaspoon ground clove

1 1/2 teaspoons salt

2 pounds boneless skinless chicken thighs, trimmed and cut into 1-inch cubes

1 teaspoon fresh lemon juice

Many curries in Kerala are flavored with a coconut-spice *masala*, but this one requires toasting the coconut and spices together before grinding them into a paste. The extra step gives this chicken curry a deep sweet flavor.

1. In a wide nonstick frying pan combine the coconut, coriander, and cayenne. Roast over medium heat, stirring constantly until the coconut turns cinnamon brown with no white remaining, and smells toasted (8 to 10 minutes). Remove it from the heat and transfer to a blender. Add 1/2 cup water and blend to a smooth paste like thick pesto; set aside. (A blender is best for this.)

2. In a Dutch oven or deep skillet, heat the oil over medium-high heat. Fry the onion until the edges begin to brown; stir in the garlic, ginger, and green chili and fry another minute. Toss in the curry leaves, dried red chili, ground masala, and salt, and fry briefly. Add the chicken pieces and stir until their pink color disappears. Now put in the coconut paste and 3/4 cup water and stir to combine. Bring to a boil; reduce the heat and simmer, covered, for 30 minutes.

3. Stir in the lemon juice and remove from heat. Check the salt and serve immediately.

PREPARATION TIME: 1 HOUR

SERVES: 6

RECIPE MAY BE PREPARED IN ADVANCE THROUGH STEP 2.

Peppery Chicken Curry

Ground masala
- 2 teaspoons coriander
- 2 teaspoons cumin
- $^{1}/_{2}$ teaspoon turmeric

$1^{1}/_{4}$ teaspoons black peppercorns, coarsely ground with a mortar and pestle

1 teaspoon salt

2 pounds boneless skinless chicken thighs, trimmed and cut into 1-inch cubes

4 tablespoons vegetable oil

2 cups sliced onion

$1^{1}/_{2}$ teaspoons minced garlic

$1^{1}/_{2}$ teaspoons minced ginger

1 teaspoon minced fresh green chili (serrano or Thai)

$^{3}/_{4}$ cup canned coconut milk

1 tablespoon Ghee (page 218) or butter

$^{1}/_{2}$ cup halved or broken raw cashews

1 teaspoon fresh lemon juice

A Christian friend, Celine Sani, served this dish to our family over twenty years ago, and my father could never forget it. The curry has a nice balance of sweet coconut milk and pungent peppercorns, but it's the cashews that are the surprise. Serve with any vegetable stir-fry and plain rice.

1. Mix together the ground masala, black pepper, and $^{1}/_{4}$ teaspoon of the salt. Rub the chicken pieces with this mixture and refrigerate for 1 hour.

2. In a wide deep nonstick pan heat the oil over medium-high heat and sauté onions until they are medium brown. Add the garlic, ginger, and green chili and fry for 1 minute. Put in the marinated chicken and remaining $^{3}/_{4}$ teaspoon salt and fry, stirring frequently until the chicken pieces lose their pink color. Stir in $^{1}/_{4}$ cup of the coconut milk and $^{1}/_{4}$ cup water, cover, and simmer for about 30 minutes over low heat.

3. Heat the ghee or butter in a frying pan. Sauté the cashews until golden brown, stirring constantly over medium heat. Set aside.

4. When the chicken is cooked add the remaining $^{1}/_{2}$ cup coconut milk. Bring to a simmer and remove from the heat. Stir in the lemon juice and taste for salt. Garnish with cashews and serve.

MARINATING TIME: 1 HOUR
PREPARATION TIME: 1 HOUR
SERVES: 6
RECIPE MAY BE PREPARED IN ADVANCE THROUGH STEP 3.

Coriander Chicken
(*Malli Char*)

4 tablespoons vegetable oil

2 cups thinly sliced onion

2 teaspoons minced garlic

2 teaspoons minced ginger

1 teaspoon minced fresh green chili (serrano or Thai)

10 to 12 fresh curry leaves

Ground masala

- 6 teaspoons coriander
- 1 teaspoon black pepper
- $^1/_2$ teaspoon cayenne
- $^1/_4$ teaspoon turmeric
- $^1/_8$ teaspoon cinnamon
- $^1/_8$ teaspoon clove
- $^1/_8$ teaspoon cardamom

$1^1/_2$ teaspoons salt

2 pounds boneless skinless chicken breasts, trimmed and cut into 1-inch cubes

$^1/_2$ cup canned coconut milk

$^1/_4$ cup chopped fresh cilantro, plus additional leaves for garnishing

This chicken recipe is another of Nimmy Paul's outstanding Syrian Christian dishes. The primary coriander flavor comes from the ground spice, but I like to add fresh coriander (cilantro) too. This curry pairs well with Coconut Rice Pancakes (page 56) for a first course. Or serve with Peppery Chickpeas (page 80), Squash with Mustard Seeds (page 72), Mung Dhal with Coconut (page 105), and plain rice.

1. In a large deep pan heat the oil over medium-high heat. Sauté the onions until the edges are nicely browned. Add the garlic, ginger, green chili, and curry leaves and fry for 1 minute.

2. Stir in the ground masala, salt, and a few teaspoons of water to prevent the spices from sticking. Fry for 2 minutes, stirring constantly.

3. Put in the chicken pieces and continue stirring over medium-high heat until the pink color disappears. Add $^1/_4$ cup of the coconut milk and $^1/_2$ cup water and bring to a boil. Reduce the heat and simmer, covered, for 20 minutes.

4. Add the remaining $^1/_4$ cup coconut milk and chopped cilantro, bring just to a boil and remove from the heat. Check the salt. Garnish with fresh cilantro leaves and serve immediately.

PREPARATION TIME: 50 MINUTES

SERVES: 6

RECIPE MAY BE PREPARED IN ADVANCE THROUGH STEP 3.

Chicken *Kurma*

1/4 cup grated unsweetened coconut

1 1/2 tablespoons raw cashew pieces

1 tablespoon white poppy seeds (optional)

5 tablespoons vegetable oil

1 1/2 cups thinly sliced shallots or onion

2 teaspoons minced garlic

2 teaspoons minced ginger

2 teaspoons finely chopped fresh green chilies (serrano or Thai)

1 cup chopped tomato

3 tablespoons coarsely chopped cilantro leaves, plus more for garnish

Ground masala
- 6 teaspoons coriander
- 1 teaspoon cumin
- 1/2 teaspoon black pepper
- 1/4 teaspoon cayenne
- 1/4 teaspoon turmeric

1 teaspoon Garam Masala (page 223)

1 1/2 teaspoons salt

2 tablespoons plain yogurt

2 pounds boneless skinless chicken thighs and breasts, trimmed and cut into 1-inch pieces

Kurma is a creamy, mild curry from North India. This is the Kerala Muslim version of the northern classic, taught to me by a Mappila woman named Haseena Sadick. Her version has rich, layered flavors and it's thickened with a coconut and cashew paste.

1. In a mini food processor or blender combine the coconut, cashews, poppy seeds, and 1/3 cup water. Grind thoroughly to form a smooth paste like pesto. (A mini food processor works best for this.) Set aside.

2. In a wide deep pan heat 3 tablespoons of the oil over medium-high heat. Fry 1 cup of the shallots until light brown. Stir in the garlic, ginger, green chili, and fry for 1 minute. Add the tomato, 3 tablespoons cilantro, ground masala, garam masala, salt, and 1/2 cup water; fry until the tomato breaks down and forms a paste.

3. Add the yogurt and stir until it dissolves. Add the chicken and bring to a boil. Reduce the heat to medium-low, cover, and simmer for 30 minutes, until the chicken is cooked through.

4. Fry the remaining 1/2 cup shallots in the remaining 2 tablespoons oil until very brown and crisp. Remove them to a plate.

5. Add the coconut and cashew paste to the chicken and simmer for 10 more minutes. Check the salt.

PREPARATION TIME: 1 HOUR 30 MINUTES
SERVES: 6
RECIPE MAY BE PREPARED IN ADVANCE THROUGH STEP 4.

Chicken with Green Chilies and Tamarind
(Chili Chicken)

$1/2$ teaspoon tamarind concentrate

7 to 10 fresh green chilies (serrano or Thai), according to taste

5 tablespoons vegetable oil

12 to 15 fresh curry leaves

$2^1/2$ cups sliced onions

2 teaspoons minced garlic

2 teaspoons minced ginger

Ground masala
- 3 teaspoons coriander
- 1 teaspoon cumin
- $1/4$ teaspoon turmeric
- $1/8$ teaspoon cayenne

1 cup chopped tomato

$1^1/4$ teaspoons salt

$1/2$ teaspoon sugar

2 pounds boneless skinless chicken thighs, trimmed and cut into 1-inch cubes

PREPARATION TIME: 1 HOUR 10 MINUTES

SERVES: 6 TO 8

RECIPE MAY BE PREPARED A DAY IN ADVANCE AND REHEATED.

A rich, piquant curry from the Jews of Kochi, who enjoyed very spicy foods like this green chili–laced curry. Because of the quantity of chilies called for, remove their seeds so their flavor can come through without the burning heat. It is not necessary to remove the chilies from the dish before serving.

1. In a small bowl combine the tamarind concentrate and 2 tablespoons hot water. Using your fingers, break up tamarind to dissolve completely.

2. If your fingers are sensitive, wear rubber gloves for this step. Remove and discard stems from the green chilies and slice in half lengthwise. With a sharp knife remove seeds and ribs; discard. Set chilies aside.

3. In a wide deep pan heat the oil over medium-high heat. Toss in the curry leaves and after they crackle for a few seconds add the onion and fry until soft. Stir in the garlic, ginger, and green chilies and fry until the onion begins to brown. Add the ground masala, tomato, salt, sugar, and $1/4$ cup water and fry until tomato breaks down and mixture becomes paste-like. Sprinkle in a little more water if the mixture dries out.

4. Put in the chicken and dissolved tamarind and simmer over medium-low heat, covered, for 35 to 40 minutes, stirring occasionally. The sauce should be moderately thick. Taste for salt before serving.

Sacks of dried red chilies in a Kochi warehouse.

Eggs with Spicy Masala
(Egg Roast)

8 large or extra large eggs

Ground masala
- 6 teaspoons coriander
- $1/2$ teaspoon cumin
- $1/4$ teaspoon turmeric
- $1/8$ teaspoon cayenne
- $1/8$ teaspoon black pepper
- $1/8$ teaspoon cinnamon
- $1/8$ teaspoon clove
- $1/8$ teaspoon cardamom

1 teaspoon fennel seeds, ground in a coffee grinder or mortar and pestle

4 tablespoons vegetable oil

$1/2$ teaspoon mustard seeds

1 dried red chili

10 to 12 fresh curry leaves

$2 1/2$ cups sliced onions

1 teaspoon salt

1 cup chopped tomatoes

$1/4$ cup canned coconut milk

PREPARATION TIME: 40 MINUTES
SERVES: 6
RECIPE MAY BE PREPARED IN ADVANCE AND REHEATED.

My aunt serves this dish with Lacy Rice Pancakes (page 50) as a light meal. Or for a main course, serve it with Spinach with Coconut (page 75), Tomato and Cucumber with Mustard Seeds (page 85), Shrimp with Cracked Pepper and Curry Leaves (page 134), and rice.

1. Bring the eggs to a boil in $1 1/2$ quarts water in a 3-quart saucepan. When the water comes to a full boil, time the eggs for 9 minutes. Remove them to a bowl of cold water. When cool, remove shells and set aside.

2. Mix the ground masala, ground fennel seeds, and $1/3$ cup water in a small bowl to make a paste.

3. In a wide nonstick frying pan heat the oil over medium-high heat. Add the mustard seeds and cover. When the seeds have popped, toss in the dried red chili and curry leaves. After the curry leaves crackle for a few seconds, put in the onion and fry until the edges turn brown.

4. Add the spice paste and salt to the onion, reduce the heat to medium and fry 3 to 4 minutes until the spices lose their raw smell, adding small amounts of water to prevent sticking. Add the tomatoes and $3/4$ cup water; simmer, stirring occasionally until tomatoes are soft and gravy is thick.

5. Stir in the coconut milk and combine thoroughly. Place the eggs in the pan and spoon the sauce over them. Bring to a simmer, cover, and keep over low heat until the eggs have warmed through. Remove from the heat and taste for salt. Serve warm.

Eggs Stirred with Coconut
(Egg *Thoren*)

8 large eggs

$1/8$ teaspoon cayenne

$1/8$ teaspoon turmeric

$1/2$ teaspoon salt

2 tablespoons vegetable oil

$1/2$ teaspoon mustard seeds

$1/4$ teaspoon cumin seeds

2 dried red chilies

8 fresh curry leaves

1 cup chopped onion

$1/4$ cup grated unsweetened coconut

My grandmother used to make this for my father when he needed quick sustenance. It's the Indian version of scrambled eggs, so I sometimes make it for brunch. It is also an easy curry to whip together if it turns out you're having more guests for dinner than expected.

1. Lightly beat the eggs with cayenne, turmeric, and salt in a bowl. Set aside.

2. In a wide nonstick frying pan heat the oil over medium-high heat. Put in the mustard seeds and cumin seeds and cover. When mustard seeds have popped, toss in the red chilies and curry leaves. After the leaves have crackled for a few seconds add the onion and sauté until soft.

3. Add the egg mixture to the oil and reduce the heat to medium. Stir gently and occasionally turn over to cook evenly. As the mixture begins to thicken, stir in the coconut. Stir periodically to form medium to large chunks. Do not overstir. When the egg is cooked through remove from the heat and serve immediately.

PREPARATION TIME: 15 MINUTES

SERVES: 6

RECIPE SHOULD BE PREPARED JUST PRIOR TO SERVING.

Minced Beef with Coconut

(Meat *Thoren*)

3/4 cup grated unsweetened coconut

Ground masala
- 4 teaspoons coriander
- 1 teaspoon cumin
- $1/2$ teaspoon cayenne
- $1/4$ teaspoon turmeric
- $1/4$ teaspoon black pepper

2 tablespoons vegetable oil

1 teaspoon mustard seeds

2 dried red chilies

10 fresh curry leaves

1 tablespoon uncooked rice

1 cup chopped onion

2 teaspoons minced garlic

2 teaspoons minced ginger

$1/2$ teaspoon minced fresh green chili
(serrano or Thai)

$1/4$ teaspoon fennel seeds, coarsely
ground with a mortar and pestle

$1 1/4$ pounds minced (not ground)
sirloin steak

2 teaspoons white vinegar

1 teaspoon salt

Beef is eaten in India in the Christian and Muslim communities where there are no religious taboos associated with it. This Syrian Christian stir-fry is a dry curry, so it's best on a menu with dishes that have sauce. Serve with Seasoned Dhal (page 104), Vegetables in Fragrant Coconut Milk (page 90), and Lime Rice (page 167).

1. In a bowl combine coconut and ground masala with $1/4$ cup water (or more) to make a moist ball. Set aside.

2. In a wok or wide deep nonstick pan heat the oil over medium-high heat. Add the mustard seeds and cover. When mustard seeds have popped, toss in the dried red chilies and curry leaves. After the curry leaves crackle for a few seconds put in the rice and fry until it turns white and puffs. Stir in the onion and fry until soft. Now add the garlic, ginger, and green chili and stir for another minute.

3. Put in the minced beef and stir frequently until the meat loses its pink color.

4. Stir in the coconut mixture, ground fennel seeds, vinegar, and salt. Continue stirring over medium heat for 5 to 8 more minutes, or until meat is completely cooked and no liquid remains. Remove from heat and check the salt. Serve warm.

PREPARATION TIME: 40 MINUTES

SERVES: 6

RECIPE MAY BE PREPARED IN ADVANCE AND REHEATED.

Spicy Beef Curry

1 1/2 pounds sirloin steak, cut into
   3/4-inch cubes or smaller

Ground masala

- 4 teaspoons coriander
- 1/2 teaspoon cumin
- 1/2 teaspoon cayenne
- 1/4 teaspoon turmeric

1/2 teaspoon fennel seeds, coarsely
   ground with a mortar and pestle

1 1/4 teaspoons salt

4 tablespoons vegetable oil

2 tablespoons Ghee (page 218)

1 (2-inch) piece cinnamon

5 whole cloves

16 to 18 fresh curry leaves (optional)

3 cups thinly sliced onion

1 1/2 teaspoons minced garlic

1 1/2 teaspoons minced ginger

1 to 2 fresh green chilies (serrano or
   Thai), split lengthwise

1/2 teaspoon fresh lemon juice

3/4 cup thinly sliced shallots or onion

PREPARATION TIME: 1 HOUR
SERVES: 6
RECIPE MAY BE PREPARED IN
   ADVANCE AND REHEATED. ADD A
   LITTLE WATER WHILE REWARMING.

Mrs. Ashraf, a friend from the Kochi area, served me her beef curry with Rice-Flour Flat Bread (page 182). Her tasty Mappila curry has a thick sauce—almost like a stir-fry. Since Indian beef can be tough, Mrs. Ashraf tenderizes the meat by boiling it first with spices.

1. In a 2-quart saucepan combine the meat, ground masala, fennel, salt, and 1/2 cup water. Bring to a boil, reduce to a simmer, cover, and cook 15 minutes. Set aside.

2. In a deep wide frying pan heat 3 tablespoons of the oil and the ghee over medium-high heat. Add the cinnamon stick and cloves and fry 2 minutes or until the spices give off their aroma. Toss in 10 or 12 curry leaves and after they have crackled for a few seconds, put in the onion. When the onion is light brown, stir in the garlic, ginger, and green chilies and continue stirring over medium-high heat until onions are browned.

3. Put in the meat and half its juices and simmer, uncovered, for 5 minutes, stirring frequently. Pour in the remaining liquid and continue frying another 5 minutes. The curry should have a thick sauce that coats the meat. Remove from the heat and add the lemon juice. Place in a serving bowl.

4. In a small frying pan heat the remaining 1 tablespoon of oil over medium-high heat. Fry the shallots until reddish brown. Add the remaining 6 to 8 curry leaves and fry until crisp. Pour over the meat as a garnish and serve immediately.

Beef in Fragrant Coconut Milk
(Meat Stew)

4 tablespoons vegetable oil

1 (2-inch) piece cinnamon, broken in two

6 whole cloves

2 cardamom pods, crushed

1/2 teaspoon peppercorns, crushed with a mortar and pestle

1 cup thinly sliced onion

6 thin slices ginger

3 fresh green chilies (serrano or Thai), split lengthwise

8 to 10 fresh curry leaves

2 pounds sirloin steak, trimmed and cut into 3/4-inch cubes

2 teaspoons all-purpose flour

1 1/2 cups canned coconut milk

1 tablespoon white vinegar

3/4 to 1 teaspoon salt

2 cups cubed (3/4-inch) peeled boiling potatoes

PREPARATION TIME: 50 MINUTES
SERVES: 6 TO 8
RECIPE MAY BE PREPARED IN ADVANCE AND GENTLY REHEATED, WITHOUT BOILING.

This aromatic meat dish has a coconut milk sauce flavored with cinnamon, clove, and cardamom. It is one of the classic dishes from the Syrian Christian community, and is usually eaten with Lacy Rice Pancakes (page 50). I recommend the combination as a first course, or for a simple meal, serve this curry with plain rice and Green Beans with Urad Dhal (page 73).

1. In a large nonstick frying pan heat the oil over medium-high heat. Add the cinnamon, cloves, cardamom, and crushed peppercorns and sauté until the spices release their fragrance (about 2 minutes). Stir in the onion, ginger, green chilies, and curry leaves and fry until the onion is soft but not brown. With a slotted spoon, remove all the ingredients to a plate, leaving behind the oil.

2. In a bowl, toss the meat pieces with the flour. Add the meat to the oil remaining in the frying pan and sauté briefly until the pink color disappears. Stir in 1/2 cup of the coconut milk, the vinegar, salt, and 1/2 cup water; simmer partly covered for 10 minutes.

3. Add the potato and previously fried ingredients. Continue simmering over medium-low heat until the potato is tender (15 to 20 minutes). Stir the mixture, breaking up cooked potato slightly to thicken the sauce.

4. Pour in the remaining 3/4 cup coconut milk, bring just to a boil and remove from heat. Taste for salt.

Spicy Chicken Liver Curry
(Liver Fry)

2 cups sliced onion

1 cup sliced shallots

1 tablespoon thinly sliced garlic

1 tablespoon thinly sliced ginger

1 green chili, split lengthwise

6 tablespoons vegetable oil

Ground masala

- 5 teaspoons coriander
- $^3/_4$ teaspoon cumin
- $^3/_4$ teaspoon cayenne, or more according to taste
- $^1/_2$ teaspoon black pepper
- $^1/_4$ teaspoon turmeric

1 teaspoon Garam Masala (page 223)

$1^1/_4$ teaspoons salt

2 pounds chicken liver, cut into 1 to $1^1/_2$-inch cubes (about 3 cups)

Here's a zesty curry from Mrs. Ashraf, a Mappila woman from central Kerala. I was startled by the heaping spoonfuls of cayenne she used, but the assertive flavor of the liver stands up to heavy spicing. My version has less cayenne, but it is still a great dish, even if you aren't a big fan of liver. Serve it with Flaky Wheat Bread (page 177).

1. In a wide skillet fry the onion, shallots, garlic, ginger, and green chili in the oil over medium-high heat until the onions brown.

2. Stir in the ground masala, garam masala, and salt; fry briefly, until the spices no longer smell raw.

3. Add the liver pieces and $^1/_2$ cup water and fry over medium-high heat, stirring often until most of the liquid evaporates, and the liver is cooked through. There should be enough sauce left to cling to the pieces of liver. Taste for salt and serve warm.

PREPARATION TIME: 40 MINUTES

SERVES: 6

RECIPE MAY BE PREPARED IN ADVANCE AND REHEATED WITH A LITTLE WATER.

Peppery Stir-Fried Lamb
(Meat Fry)

2 pounds boned leg of lamb or
   marbled beef (sirloin), cut into
   $3/4$-inch cubes

Ground masala
  • 4 teaspoons coriander
  • $1/2$ teaspoon cayenne
  • $1/4$ teaspoon turmeric
  • $1/8$ teaspoon cinnamon
  • $1/8$ teaspoon clove
  • $1/8$ teaspoon cardamom

$1/4$ teaspoon fennel seeds, coarsely
   ground with a mortar and pestle

$1^{1}/_{2}$ teaspoons salt

3 teaspoons white vinegar

5 tablespoons vegetable oil

2 cups thinly sliced onion

3 teaspoons minced ginger

2 teaspoons minced garlic

2 teaspoons peppercorns, crushed
   with a mortar and pestle

$3/4$ cup Coconut Slices (page 220)

$1/2$ cup sliced shallots or onion

8 to 10 fresh curry leaves

This is a flavorful Syrian Christian curry with crunchy chips of coconut mixed into its thick sauce. The coconut slices can be omitted, but the curry is tastier with them. This dish is excellent with Spicy Fried Tomatoes (page 69), Sweet Green Mango Chutney (page 191), Mung Dhal with Coconut (page 105), and plain rice.

1. In a large deep nonstick pan combine the meat, ground masala, fennel, salt, vinegar, and $1/2$ cup water. Bring to a boil then reduce heat to low. Cover and simmer for 20 minutes, until the meat is no longer pink inside. With a slotted spoon, remove the meat to a plate. Pour the meat juices into a separate bowl and reserve (about 1 cup).

2. Using the same pan, wiped clean, heat 4 tablespoons of the oil over medium-high heat. Sauté 2 cups of sliced onion until light brown. Stir in the ginger, garlic, and crushed peppercorns and fry for a minute. Add the meat pieces and $1/4$ cup of the reserved juices, sautéing over medium-high heat until the liquid has mostly evaporated. Repeat this process, adding a $1/4$ cup of reserved juices at a time and stirring continually after each addition, until the last addition of liquid thickens to form a creamy coating on the meat. This process tenderizes the meat and darkens the sauce, and should take about 15 minutes. Use water if you run out of liquid and the mixture looks too dry. Remove from the heat and spoon into a serving bowl.

3. In a small frying pan heat the remaining 1 tablespoon of oil and fry the coconut slices, the shallots (or onion), and curry leaves until the shallots are crisp and brown. Pour this mixture over meat as a garnish and serve immediately.

PREPARATION AND COOKING TIME: 50 MINUTES

SERVES: 6

RECIPE MAY BE PREPARED IN ADVANCE THROUGH STEP 2. ADD A LITTLE WATER WHEN REHEATING.

Lamb *Vindaloo*

4 tablespoons vegetable oil

2 cups thinly sliced onion

1¹/₂ teaspoons minced garlic

1¹/₂ teaspoons minced ginger

2 tablespoons minced golden raisins

2¹/₂ tablespoons white vinegar

Ground masala

- 1¹/₂ teaspoons cayenne
- 1 teaspoon cumin
- ¹/₂ teaspoon coriander
- ¹/₄ teaspoon turmeric
- ¹/₈ teaspoon cinnamon
- ¹/₈ teaspoon clove

1 teaspoon mustard seeds, finely ground with a mortar and pestle

1³/₄ teaspoons salt

2 pounds boned leg of lamb, trimmed of fat, cut into ³/₄-inch cubes

This classic hot and sour curry comes from Goa, but my friend Nimmy Paul of Kochi has such an interesting version I included it. She uses raisins to balance the pungency of the cayenne and vinegar. The lamb can be replaced with lean beef or pork if you prefer. Have it with Carrots with Coconut (page 77), Cucumber with Black-eyed Peas (page 89), Thoor Dhal with Tomato and Onion (page 106), and plain rice.

1. In a deep frying pan with a lid heat the oil over medium-high heat. Add the onion and fry until the edges are nicely browned. Stir in the garlic and ginger and fry another minute.

2. Add the minced raisins, vinegar, ground masala, ground mustard seeds, salt, and ¹/₄ cup water. Fry, stirring, for 3 minutes or until the spices lose their raw smell. Put in the meat and another ¹/₄ cup water and bring to a boil, stirring constantly. Reduce the heat to low, cover, and cook for 35 minutes. Uncover, increase the heat to medium-high, and continue to simmer, stirring occasionally for 10 more minutes or until the sauce thickens and the meat becomes tender. There should be plenty of thick sauce. Taste for salt and serve warm.

PREPARATION TIME: 1 HOUR 30 MINUTES

SERVES: 6

RECIPE MAY BE PREPARED A DAY IN ADVANCE AND REHEATED.

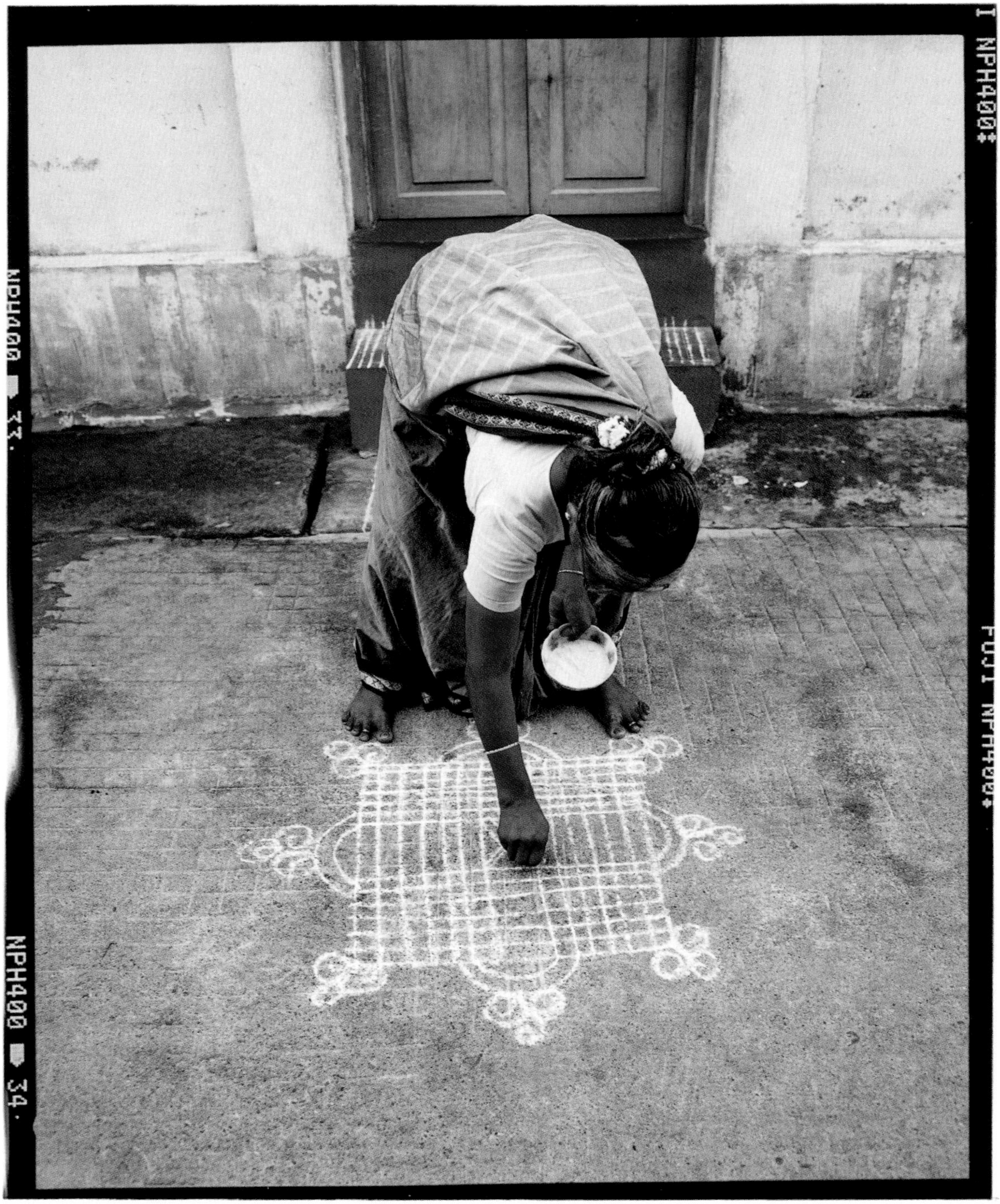
I NPH400
FUJI NPH400
NPH400 33.
NPH400 34.

Rice and Breads

Rice is one of Kerala's most important crops. Of the many varieties cultivated there, rosematta is the one preferred for eating with curries. It has plump, bouncy grains flecked with red bran, and has been commercially par-boiled to force the nutrients from the bran into the kernel. At home it's boiled (like pasta) in a large amount of water until tender. When drained, the rice grains are round and separate and have a faintly meaty aroma. Since nothing is wasted in India, the cooking water, called *kanjee,* is consumed as a restorative broth.

Long-grain rice is generally reserved for pancake and dumpling batters in South India, but it can also be steamed and served plain with the curries in this book, especially since rosematta is not yet widely available in the United States. Another excellent rice for eating with curries is basmati, an aromatic rice that is grown along the foothills of the North Indian Himalayan mountains.

A Brahmin woman performs a daily ritual, decorating the entrance to her home with rice flour.

Basmati has delicate long grains and is aged for at least a year after it's harvested in order to improve the flavor. Everyone eats basmati in the North, but in the South it's primarily the Mappilas (Kerala Muslims) who cook with it. Mappilas use this rice in their *biriyani*, the elegant baked casserole with alternating layers of rice and spiced meat, fish, or vegetable, which is baked under hot coals (or in an oven) so the flavors can mingle as the different components steam together.

Biriyani is originally a North Indian Muslim dish, but it was adopted by the Muslims in the South, who added local elements like coconut and curry leaves to their exceptional rendition of this classic. In Kerala non-Muslims covet invitations to Mappila weddings for the chance to eat their renowned mutton *biriyani*. ("Mutton" in India refers to goat meat although we know it as lamb.) While mutton is the most popular type of *biriyani* in the Mappila community, the shrimp and fish versions are quite wonderful too.

Alongside the *biriyani* and curries eaten at midday, Muslims usually serve a type of fresh bread, or *pathiri*. These delectable breads range in complexity from flat breads to decoratively folded individual yeast breads. Many of the *pathiri* are deep-fried, adding to their richness, and they can turn an ordinary meal into an uncommon one.

Simple wheat flat breads such as *chappathis* and *puris* might be served with one or two thick curries for dinner in lieu of rice in a Muslim, Christian, or Hindu home. *Parathas* are a favorite in my aunt's house: they have layers of ghee (clarified butter) brushed into the dough when it is rolled, giving them a flaky texture. This is an easy bread to prepare, and quite delicious.

There are no hard rules about what type of starch to serve with South Indian food. If you want to keep your meal planning simple, serve plain rice. But if you wish to be more elaborate, add a fresh bread and/or serve a luscious *biriyani*.

Boiled Rosematta Rice
Steamed Long-Grain Rice
Steamed Basmati Rice
Lime Rice
Ghee Rice
Lamb *Biriyani*
Fish *Biriyani*
Shrimp *Biriyani*
Seeded Yeast Bread (*Kameer*)
Flaky Wheat Bread (*Paratha*)
Puffy White Bread Pockets (*Maida Bathura*)
Puffed Bread with "Eyes" (*Kannan Pathiri*)
Rice-Flour Flat Bread (*Podi Pathiri*)

Boiled Rosematta Rice

2 cups rosematta rice

1 teaspoon salt

Rosematta is a red-tinted rice with a faintly meaty aroma that is grown and eaten in Kerala. When harvested, the rice is pre-boiled while still in its reddish husks, so some of the bran and color remain on the grains. In Kerala people prefer to boil this rice in a lot of water, like pasta, for the plumpest, tenderest texture. Rosematta is not widely available in America yet, but it is sold at some Indian and Asian markets.

1. Place the rice in a bowl and rinse it in many changes of cold water until the water no longer appears cloudy. Drain.

2. In a large stockpot bring 12 cups water and the salt to a boil. Add the drained rice, bring back to a boil, and stir. Reduce the heat slightly, keeping the water at a steady boil. Time it for 20 minutes.

3. After 20 minutes, test a few grains to see if they are tender. If not, boil it for a few more minutes. When tender, drain the rice in a colander and briefly rinse with lukewarm water. The grains will be firm, rounded, and separate from each other. Serve immediately.

COOKING TIME: 25 MINUTES

SERVES: 6

Steamed Long-Grain Rice

2 cups long-grain rice
1 teaspoon salt

1. In a heavy 3-quart pot with a tight-fitting lid bring 1 quart water to a boil. Add the rice and salt, stirring to break up any lumps.

2. When the water returns to a boil, turn the heat down to low, cover, and simmer for 35 minutes, or until all the water has been absorbed. Do not remove the lid and do not stir during this period.

3. Fluff the cooked rice with a fork and serve hot.

COOKING TIME: 35 MINUTES
SERVES: 6

Steamed Basmati Rice

2 cups basmati rice

1 teaspoon salt

There are various methods for cooking this aromatic grain, but this is the one I prefer. It produces nice separate grains if the rice is well drained before boiling; otherwise it becomes mushy.

1. Wash the basmati rice in a bowl with many changes of cold water until the water no longer appears cloudy. Remove any debris. Drain the rice *thoroughly*.

2. Place the rice, salt, and $3^{1}/_{2}$ cups water in a heavy 3-quart pot with a tight-fitting lid over high heat. When it boils, reduce the heat to very low, cover, and simmer for 20 minutes. Do not stir or remove the lid.

3. Remove the pot from the heat and allow to rest, covered, for another 10 minutes. Fluff the rice with a fork and serve hot.

COOKING TIME: 35 MINUTES

SERVES: 6

Lime Rice

2 1/2 teaspoons salt

2 cups long-grain rice (not basmati)

2 teaspoons Ghee (page 218) or butter

1/3 cup broken cashew pieces

1/4 cup vegetable oil

1 teaspoon mustard seeds

2 dried red chilies

15 fresh curry leaves

2 tablespoons channa dhal or yellow split peas

2 tablespoons urad dhal

1/4 teaspoon turmeric

1/8 teaspoon ground asafetida

1 teaspoon minced fresh green chili (serrano or Thai)

5 tablespoons fresh lime juice

PREPARATION TIME: 35 MINUTES
SERVES: 6
RECIPE MAY BE PREPARED AN HOUR IN ADVANCE THROUGH STEP 4. KEEP WARM.

This pretty rice dish with lime juice and cashews and crunchy fried dhal goes well with fish and shrimp curries. I suggest using long-grain rice instead of basmati, which has a very distinct aroma that is not appropriate for this dish. Always add the lime juice just before serving so its flavor doesn't fade.

1. In a heavy 2-quart pot with a tight-fitting lid bring a scant quart of water and 1 1/2 teaspoons of the salt to a boil. Add the rice, return to a boil, and reduce the heat to low. Cover tightly and cook for 25 minutes.

2. Meanwhile, in a wide frying pan heat the ghee. Add the cashew pieces and fry until nicely browned. Remove the cashews to a plate, but leave any ghee behind in the pan.

3. To the same pan add the oil and turn the heat to medium. Add the mustard seeds and cover. When the seeds have popped, toss in the dried red chilies and curry leaves. After the leaves have crackled for a few seconds add the dhals and fry until they just begin to color. Stir in the turmeric, asafetida, green chili, and the remaining 1 teaspoon salt; fry for 1 minute. Remove from the heat.

4. Fluff the cooked rice with a fork. Pour the sautéed seasonings and their oil over the rice and stir to combine thoroughly.

5. Add the lime juice and stir. Spread the rice on a platter and garnish with the cashews. Serve warm.

Ghee Rice

2 cups basmati rice

$1/4$ cup Ghee (page 218)

2 cups thinly sliced onions

1 (2-inch) piece cinnamon, broken in
   two

4 whole cloves

4 cardamom pods, crushed

$1^1/_2$ teaspoons salt

Many Mappilas (Kerala Muslims) prefer their rice seasoned this way rather than plain. This buttery, slightly perfumed rice is good with Chicken *Kurma* (page 147), Chicken with Green Chilies and Tamarind (page 148), Spicy Chicken Liver Curry (page 155), or Lamb *Vindaloo* (page 159).

1. In a large bowl wash the rice in many changes of water until the water no longer appears cloudy. Drain thoroughly.

2. In a heavy pot with a tight-fitting lid heat the ghee. Add the onions, cinnamon, cloves, and cardamom. Fry until the onions brown along the edges. Put in the drained rice and sauté for about 2 minutes, or until the grains of rice begin to jump on the bottom of the pan.

3. Add $3^1/_4$ cups boiling water and the salt and bring to a rolling boil. Reduce the heat to low, cover, and steam for 20 minutes. Remove from the heat and allow to sit, covered, for 10 minutes. Serve warm.

PREPARATION TIME: 45 MINUTES

SERVES: 6

RECIPE MAY BE PREPARED IN ADVANCE THROUGH STEP 1.

Huge aluminum vessels are used to hold water; smaller ones to cook rice and curries.

Lamb *Biriyani*

Masala

3/4 cup grated unsweetened coconut

2 teaspoons white poppy seeds (optional)

10 to 12 fresh curry leaves (optional)

1 to 2 teaspoons chopped fresh green chili (serrano or Thai), according to taste

3 tablespoons vegetable oil

3 tablespoons Ghee (page 218)

3 cups thinly sliced onions

1 tablespoon minced garlic

1 tablespoon minced ginger

Ground masala
  - 2 teaspoons coriander
  - 1 teaspoon cumin
  - 1/2 teaspoon black pepper
  - 1/4 teaspoon cayenne

1 1/2 teaspoons Garam Masala (page 223)

2 teaspoons salt

1/4 cup plain yogurt

2 tablespoons fresh lime juice

1/2 cup chopped fresh cilantro

1/2 cup chopped fresh mint

2 pounds boned leg of lamb, cut into 3/4-inch cubes (about 4 cups)

Biriyani, a rice and meat casserole, came to India from Central Asia by way of the Mughals, who ruled much of India from the sixteenth to eighteenth centuries. To this day it is considered one of India's most elegant dishes, and is particularly popular in North India. This version, with South Indian touches like coconut and curry leaves, is the pride of the Mappila (Kerala Muslim) community, and a mainstay at Muslim weddings. This is Mrs. Ashraf's recipe, although I substitute lamb for the goat meat that she uses. For an elaborate dinner, serve this *biriyani* with a fish or chicken curry, and one or two vegetable dishes, Tomato and Cucumber Salad (page 194), and Puffy White Bread Pockets (page 178).

1. In a blender or mini food processor combine the coconut, poppy seeds, curry leaves, green chili, and 1/2 cup water (or more) to make a paste like thick pesto. Set aside.

2. Heat 3 tablespoons oil and 3 tablespoons ghee in a wide frying pan over medium-high heat. Add 3 cups onions and sauté until the edges are lightly browned. Put in the garlic and ginger and continue frying about 3 minutes, until you smell the aroma and the onions are brown. Stir in the ground masala, garam masala, salt, and coconut paste and fry for 2 to 3 minutes. Add the yogurt, lime juice, cilantro, and mint. Stir over medium-high heat for 2 to 3 minutes. Now put in the lamb pieces and stir. When the mixture comes to a boil, reduce the heat, cover, and simmer for 30 to 40 minutes, until the meat is tender. Stir occasionally.

3. In a large bowl, wash the rice in many changes of water until the water no longer appears cloudy. Drain thoroughly.

4. Prepare the garnish by heating 2 tablespoons oil and 2 tablespoons ghee in a frying pan. Add the 2 cups onions and fry over medium-high heat, stirring constantly, until they turn deep reddish brown and crisp (10 to 15 minutes). Remove the onions to a plate with a slotted spoon. Fry the cashews in the remaining oil until brown. Remove the nuts with a slotted spoon and repeat with the raisins. Set aside.

5. Prepare the rice by combining the 2 teaspoons salt, the drained rice, and 5 cups water in a large heavy pan with a tight-fitting lid. Bring to a boil, cover, and simmer 20 minutes on low heat. Remove from the heat.

6. Preheat the oven to 350 degrees F.

7. Fluff the rice and spread one third of it in the bottom of a casserole or Dutch oven with a tight-fitting lid. Sprinkle one third of the fried onions, cashews, and raisins on top of rice, then add half the lamb mixture. Continue to layer with one third of the rice, one third of the garnish, all the remaining lamb, and finally the last third of rice. Reserve the last third of the garnish for later. Seal the top with foil, then place the lid over the foil. Bake for 30 minutes.

8. Spoon onto a large platter and garnish with the remaining fried onions, cashews, and raisins. Place the halved boiled eggs, yolk up, around the edges of the platter. Serve immediately.

PREPARATION TIME: 1¹/₂ HOURS
BAKING TIME: 30 MINUTES
SERVES: 8 TO 10
RECIPE MAY BE PREPARED IN ADVANCE THROUGH STEP 4.

Rice
3 cups basmati rice
2 teaspoons salt
Garnish
2 tablespoons vegetable oil
2 tablespoons Ghee (page 218)
2 cups thinly sliced onions
1/2 cup broken cashew pieces
1/2 cup golden raisins
4 large hard-boiled eggs, halved

Fish *Biriyani*

Marinade

$1/4$ teaspoon cayenne

$1/8$ teaspoon turmeric

$1/4$ teaspoon fennel seeds, finely
   ground with a mortar and pestle

$1/8$ teaspoon salt

$1^1/2$ pounds fish fillets (haddock or
   cod), skin on

2 tablespoons vegetable oil

Masala

4 tablespoons vegetable oil

2 cups sliced onions

$1^1/2$ teaspoons minced garlic

$1^1/2$ teaspoons minced ginger

$1^1/2$ teaspoons minced green chili

1 cup chopped tomato

Ground masala

- 2 teaspoons coriander
- $1/2$ teaspoon cumin
- $1/4$ teaspoon cayenne
- $1/4$ teaspoon turmeric
- $1/8$ teaspoon black pepper

$1/2$ teaspoon Garam Masala
   page 223)

$3/4$ teaspoon salt

2 tablespoons plain yogurt

2 teaspoons lime juice

$1/4$ cup chopped fresh cilantro

$1/4$ cup chopped fresh mint

Although not as popular as meat *biriyani*, the fish version is another treasure of the Mappila community. This stunning fish and rice casserole was shown to me by Haseena Sadick of Kochi. As *biriyani* can be a time-consuming project, she cooked the fish in its slightly sour tomato masala ahead of time. Have this *biriyani* with Yogurt Salad (page 195), Peppery Chickpeas (page 80), Green Coconut Chutney (page 190), and Puffed Bread with "Eyes" (page 180).

1. To prepare the marinade, combine the cayenne, turmeric, fennel, and salt. Cut the fish into large pieces that won't break apart (about 2 x 2 inches). Rub the fish pieces with the spice mixture. Marinate 10 to 15 minutes. (This step helps draw the liquid out of the fish so it holds together during cooking.)

2. Heat 2 tablespoons oil in a nonstick frying pan and fry the fish pieces until they change color but do not become crisp (about 2 minutes on each side). Set aside.

3. Using the same pan, wiped clean, heat 4 tablespoons oil over medium-high heat. Sauté the onions until the edges are nicely browned. Add the garlic, ginger, and green chili and fry for 1 minute. Stir in the tomato, ground masala, garam masala, salt, and $1/2$ cup water. Fry for 2 to 3 minutes or until the tomato begins to soften. Add the yogurt, lime juice, cilantro, and mint and stir until well blended.

4. Carefully add the fish pieces to the pan, spooning the sauce over them. Reduce the heat to low, cover, and simmer for 10

minutes. Swirl the pan from time to time to circulate the sauce, but do not stir or the fish will break apart. Taste for salt. The sauce should look thick and taste a little sour.

5. Place the rice in a large bowl and rinse with changes of cold water until the water no longer appears cloudy. Drain thoroughly in a strainer.

6. To make the garnish, heat 2 tablespoons oil and the ghee in a frying pan. Fry 1 cup onion slowly over medium heat, stirring constantly, until the onion turns reddish brown and crisp (10 to 15 minutes); remove it to a plate. In the remaining oil, fry the cashews until golden brown. Remove and repeat with the raisins, until they become plump and golden brown. Set aside.

7. To prepare the rice, bring 3½ cups water to a boil in a saucepan. Cover and keep over a very low flame.

8. In a large pot with tight-fitting lid, heat the 2 tablespoons oil. Add the cinnamon, cloves, and cardamom, and sauté for 1 minute, or until the spices give off their aroma. Add the drained rice and stir over medium heat until the rice begins to jump slightly in the pan. Add the boiling water and salt and stir. Reduce the heat to low, cover tightly, and cook for 20 minutes until tender.

9. Preheat the oven to 350 degrees F.

10. When the rice is done, fluff it and spread half of it in a heavy casserole or Dutch oven (with a tight-fitting lid). Sprinkle one third of the fried onion over the rice, then add all the fish pieces and half their sauce. Add the rest of the rice, another third of the fried onion, and the remaining sauce. Seal the top with foil, then place the lid over the foil. Bake for 15 minutes.

11. Carefully transfer the rice and fish to a platter, being careful not to break up the fish pieces. Sprinkle with the fried onion, cashews, and raisins. Serve immediately.

Rice

2 cups basmati rice
2 tablespoons vegetable oil
1 (2-inch) piece cinnamon
3 whole cloves
2 cardamom pods, crushed
1 teaspoon salt

Garnish

2 tablespoons vegetable oil
1 tablespoon Ghee (page 218)
1 cup sliced onion
¼ cup raw cashews (optional)
¼ cup golden raisins (optional)

A fish seller near the port of Kozhikode.

PREPARATION TIME: 1½ HOURS
BAKING TIME: 15 MINUTES
SERVES: 6
RECIPE MAY BE PREPARED IN
 ADVANCE THROUGH STEP 6.

Shrimp *Biriyani*

Masala

¹/₄ cup grated unsweetened coconut

1 tablespoon white poppy seeds
  (optional)

1¹/₂ tablespoons raw cashews

3 tablespoons vegetable oil

¹/₂ teaspoon peppercorns, crushed
  with a mortar and pestle

2 cups thinly sliced onions

2 teaspoons minced garlic

2 teaspoons minced ginger

1 teaspoon minced green chili
  (serrano or Thai)

1 cup chopped tomato

Ground masala
  • 3 teaspoons coriander
  • 1 teaspoon cumin
  • ¹/₄ teaspoon cayenne
  • ¹/₄ teaspoon turmeric

¹/₂ teaspoon Garam Masala
  (page 223)

1¹/₄ teaspoons salt

¹/₄ cup plain yogurt

1 tablespoon fresh lime juice

3 tablespoons chopped fresh cilantro

3 tablespoons chopped fresh mint

1 pound extra-large or jumbo shrimp,
  peeled and deveined

This is another great Mappila casserole: it marries fragrant rice with shrimp cooked in a creamy, piquant sauce. *Biriyanis* are eaten throughout India, but this one with shrimp and coconut has the unmistakable stamp of Kerala.

1. In a mini food processor or blender combine the coconut, white poppy seeds, cashews, and ¹/₃ cup water. Blend on high speed for about 3 minutes, stopping to scrape ingredients off the sides. It should be the texture of creamy pesto. (A mini food processor works best for this.) Set aside.

2. In a deep wide nonstick pan heat the oil over medium-high heat. Toss in the crushed peppercorns and fry for 1 minute. Add the onions and fry until the edges are nicely browned. Stir in the garlic, ginger, and green chili and fry for 2 minutes or until the seasonings release their aroma, and the onions are well browned. Add the tomato, ground masala, garam masala, salt, and ¹/₂ cup water and fry until the tomato begins to break down. Now stir in the coconut paste and fry for 2 minutes until the mixture darkens and the oil separates. It should resemble a thick paste.

3. Add the yogurt, lime juice, cilantro, and mint. Bring to a simmer and add ³/₄ cup water and the shrimp. Stir until the shrimp just lose their translucent quality and are barely cooked through. The sauce should be a bit thick. Remove from the heat and set aside, covered.

4. In a large bowl, wash the rice in many changes of water until the water no longer appears cloudy. Drain thoroughly.

5. Prepare the garnish by heating the vegetable oil and ghee in a frying pan. Over medium heat fry 1 cup onion, stirring constantly until it turns deep reddish brown and crisp (about 10 minutes). Remove the onion to a plate with a slotted spoon. Fry the cashews in the remaining oil until brown. Set aside.

6. Bring $3^{1}/_{2}$ cups water, the salt, and the drained rice to a boil in a heavy-bottomed 2-quart pot with a tight-fitting lid. Reduce the heat to low, cover, and steam 20 minutes. Turn off the heat, and allow to sit 10 minutes with the cover on.

7. Preheat the oven to 350 degrees F.

8. Fluff the cooked rice with a fork and place half of it in a Dutch oven or heavy casserole, forming an even layer. With a slotted spoon, remove the shrimp from the sauce and place them over the rice. Add the rest of the rice, and evenly distribute the remaining sauce on top of it. Seal the top with foil, then place the lid over the foil. Bake 15 minutes.

9. When the rice has finished baking, gently blend the ingredients together. Serve garnished with the fried onions, cashews, and chopped cilantro. Serve immediately.

PREPARATION TIME: $1^{1}/_{2}$ HOURS
BAKING TIME: 15 MINUTES
SERVES: 6
RECIPE MAY BE PREPARED IN ADVANCE THROUGH STEP 5.

Rice
2 cups basmati rice
1 teaspoon salt
Garnish
1 tablespoon vegetable oil
1 tablespoon Ghee (page 218)
1 cup thinly sliced onion
$^{1}/_{4}$ cup broken cashews
2 tablespoons coarsely chopped fresh cilantro

Seeded Yeast Bread
(Kameer)

2 teaspoons active dry yeast

2 cups all-purpose flour

2 teaspoons black sesame seeds (or white)

4 teaspoons sugar

1/2 teaspoon salt

1 large egg yolk

Vegetable oil for deep-frying

PREPARATION TIME: 30 MINUTES

RISING TIME: 1 1/2 HOURS

COOKING TIME: 20 MINUTES

SERVES: 6

YIELD: 12

RECIPE MAY BE PREPARED HALF AN HOUR IN ADVANCE THROUGH STEP 3.

This Mappila (Kerala Muslim) yeast bread is flecked with black sesame seeds. It is excellent with chicken or meat curries with gravy, such as Chicken *Kurma* (page 147), Beef in Fragrant Coconut Milk (page 154), or Lamb *Vindaloo* (page 159).

1. In a small bowl combine the yeast with 1/2 cup barely warm water. Set aside for 10 minutes, until it appears foamy.

2. In a large bowl blend the flour, sesame seeds, sugar, and salt. Add the proofed yeast and the egg yolk. Gradually add enough water (about 1/3 cup) to make a manageable dough. Knead it 5 to 10 minutes until smooth and soft. Put it in an oiled bowl and place somewhere warm (an oven with a large bowl of hot water) to rise for 1 1/2 hours.

3. When the dough has tripled in size, punch it down and divide into twelve equal-sized balls. On a floured surface, roll out each to a thin disk, about 1/8 inch thick and 5 inches in diameter.

4. Heat about 2 inches of oil in a wok to 350 degrees F. (Oil is hot enough when a tiny ball of dough dropped into it immediately pops to the surface.) Carefully slide one disk into the hot oil. The *kameer* will develop large air bubbles and then puff up like a balloon, at which point it should be turned three or four times until golden brown. Remove to drain on a paper towel and repeat. These breads stay puffy as they cool but should be served immediately.

Flaky Wheat Bread
(Paratha)

2 cups *atta* (*chappathi* flour)

1 teaspoon salt

$^1/_4$ cup Ghee (page 218)

This flat bread is popular in North and South India alike. A little ghee brushed into the dough makes it flaky. The bread goes well with thick curries like Chickpeas with Onion (page 78) or Spicy Chicken Liver Curry (page 155).

1. In a bowl combine the flour and salt. Gradually add $^3/_4$ to 1 cup warm water until all the flour is incorporated. Knead in the bowl for a few minutes to form a soft dough. Set aside, covered, for 15 minutes.

2. Knead the dough again and divide into $1^1/_2$-inch balls. On a lightly floured surface, roll each ball out to a thin 6-inch disk. Brush about $^1/_4$ teaspoon ghee on each disk without touching the edges. Fold the disk in half, then in half again. Seal the edges by pressing them together with your fingers. Sprinkle with flour and roll out again, forming a 6- to 7-inch triangle. Set the triangle on a lightly floured surface, cover with a cloth, and repeat with each of the remaining disks.

3. Heat an Indian *tava* (iron griddle) or heavy cast-iron skillet over medium heat. When a few particles of flour sprinkled on the skillet turn light brown, it's hot enough for frying. Frying one a time, place a *paratha* on the skillet, and using a folded paper towel press it lightly. When the underside has brown spots, flip it and fry the other side until browned, brushing the top with a little ghee. Remove to a work surface and lightly brush the other side with ghee. Wrap in foil to keep warm until all the *parathas* are cooked. Serve promptly.

RESTING TIME: 15 MINUTES

COOKING TIME: 25 MINUTES

YIELD: 16

RECIPE MAY BE PREPARED HALF AN HOUR IN ADVANCE THROUGH STEP 2.

Puffy White Bread Pockets
(Maida Bathura)

1/2 teaspoon active dry yeast
4 teaspoons sugar
2 cups all-purpose flour
2 teaspoons Ghee (page 218)
1 large egg yolk, lightly beaten
1/2 teaspoon salt
Vegetable oil for deep-frying

Although this rich yeast bread is commonly found in North India, Muslims in Kerala make it to eat with Chicken *Kurma* (page 147). It also goes nicely with Peppery Chicken Curry (page 144) or Beef in Fragrant Coconut Milk (page 154).

1. In a small bowl combine 1/4 cup barely warm water with the yeast and 1 teaspoon of the sugar. Set aside for 10 minutes, until it appears foamy.

2. In a mixing bowl blend the flour and ghee with your hands for about 5 minutes, or until the mixture resembles coarse meal.

3. Add the proofed yeast, egg yolk, remaining 3 teaspoons sugar, and the salt and continue to mix by hand. Gradually sprinkle in enough water, 1/4 to 1/2 cup, to make a soft, barely sticky dough. Turn onto a lightly floured surface and knead 5 to 10 minutes to form a very smooth dough.

4. Place the dough in a lightly oiled bowl, cover with a damp cloth, and keep in a warm place (an oven with a large bowl of hot water) for an hour to rise.

5. When doubled in size, knead the dough a few times and divide into twelve equal-size balls. On a lightly floured surface, roll out the balls with a rolling pin into 4- to 5-inch disks, 1/4 inch thick. (If too thin they will form holes when fried.) Keep the disks covered with a moist towel.

6. Place about 2 inches of oil in a wok and heat to 350 degrees F. (The oil is hot enough when a tiny ball of dough dropped

into it immediately pops to the surface.) Drop one disk into the oil, spooning oil over the top until it puffs into a balloon. Turn a few times until both sides are golden brown. Remove to a paper towel and repeat with the rest. The bread deflates slightly, so serve immediately.

PREPARATION TIME: 25 MINUTES
RISING TIME: 1 HOUR
FRYING TIME: 20 MINUTES
SERVES: 4 TO 6
YIELD: 12
RECIPE MAY BE PREPARED HALF AN HOUR IN ADVANCE THROUGH STEP 5.

Puffed Bread with "Eyes"
(Kannan Pathiri)

1 cup all-purpose flour
1 cup *atta* (*chappathi* flour)
¼ teaspoon salt
2 teaspoons vegetable oil, plus more
   for deep-frying

The name translates as "eye bread" because the folds form a pattern on top that looks like eyes. Aside from being attractive, these breads are very tasty and go especially well with Chicken *Kurma* (page 147), Spicy Beef Curry (page 153), or Lamb *Vindaloo* (page 159).

1. In a bowl combine the flours, salt, and 2 teaspoons oil and mix together using your fingers. Gradually add small amounts of warm water, mixing the dough with your hand. Add just enough water to moisten the flour and form a stiff dough. Turn the dough out onto a clean surface and knead for 5 to 10 minutes until it becomes smooth and silky.

2. Divide the dough into sixteen (1-inch) balls. Lightly flour the surface with all-purpose flour and with a rolling pin roll each ball out to a thin disk, about 6 inches in diameter. Brush the top side lightly with oil. Fold two opposite sides in toward the center so their curved sides touch. Then fold the other two sides in, forming a square. Take each corner and fold it into the center, forming an even smaller square. Press flat with the heel of your hand. Turn the square over so the folded side is facing down, and with the rolling pin, roll out to a 4-inch square. Continue with the remaining balls, keeping the rolled dough covered.

3. In a small wok or frying pan heat about 2 inches of oil to 350 degrees F. Test by dropping a tiny piece of dough in the oil. If it bobs to the top immediately, the oil is hot enough. Fry each

pathiri, one at a time, in the hot oil. Turn frequently until both sides are a deep golden brown color, and the surface is slightly bubbly. Remove to drain on paper towels. Serve immediately.

PREPARATION TIME: 25 MINUTES
COOKING TIME: 15 MINUTES
SERVES: 6
YIELD: 16
RECIPE MAY BE PREPARED HALF AN HOUR IN ADVANCE THROUGH STEP 2.

Puffed Bread with "Eyes" before the final rolling (above) and after being fried.

Rice-Flour Flat Bread
(Podi Pathiri)

1 teaspoon salt
1 cup rice flour, plus additional rice
    flour for rolling
1 cup canned coconut milk

Pathiri is the generic word for bread among Kerala Muslims. These are basic rice-flour flat breads, similar to *chappathis*. They have a slightly dry texture, so the usual way to eat them is to dip or soak them in coconut milk. Serve with Spicy Beef Curry (page 153) or Peppery Stir-Fried Lamb (page 156).

1. In a saucepan bring 2 cups water to a boil. Remove $1/2$ cup and keep warm for later. Stir the salt into the saucepan and remove from the heat. Slowly add the rice flour, stirring constantly with a fork. The mixture should be damp enough to form a clump when pressed together, but not stick to your fingers. Add some of the reserved water if the dough is dry. (If it's too dry the *pathiri* will crack around the edges when cooked.) Turn onto a floured surface for kneading.

2. Knead the dough into a ball. It should be moist but not sticky.

3. After forming a smooth ball, roll the dough into $1 1/2$-inch balls between the palms of your hands. Dip a ball in the additional rice flour and place it on a lightly floured surface. With a rolling pin roll out to a flat, extremely thin disk, about $1/16$ inch thick and 6 inches in diameter. Roll the remaining balls in the same manner, keeping them covered with a cloth.

4. Heat a *tava* (iron griddle) or cast-iron skillet over medium heat. When hot place a disk in the center. After 15 to 20 seconds flip it over. Continue to flip occasionally until dry white patches appear. Press down slightly with a folded paper

towel, forcing the *pathiri* to puff slightly. Remove it when pale brown spots appear. Repeat with the other disks, again keeping the uncooked *pathiris* covered so they do not dry out.

5. When all the *pathiris* are cooked, place the coconut milk in a bowl and dip them, two at a time, into the bowl. Holding them together, let the liquid drip off, then roll them into a cylinder, and place them on a platter. Continue with the next two, laying them next to the first set on the platter. Alternately, place the first *pathiri* on a plate and brush the top surface with coconut milk. Place the second directly on top of the first, and brush it with more coconut milk. Repeat with the remaining *pathiris*.
Serve immediately.

PREPARATION TIME: 25 MINUTES
COOKING TIME: 20 MINUTES
YIELD: 16
SERVES: 4 TO 6
RECIPE MAY BE PREPARED HALF AN HOUR IN ADVANCE THROUGH STEP 3.

Ladling Rice-Flour Flat Breads with coconut milk.

Chutneys, Pickles, and Salads

Indians crave an array of intense flavors on the same plate, so alongside their curries, they like to have one or two zesty condiments to liven up the meal. A uniquely Indian relish is the chutney, a mixture of fruits, herbs, and spices, which can be made fresh or cooked and jarred, as with the popular Major Grey's brand of chutney. Pickles are more intensely flavored condiments made from fruit, vegetables, fish, or meat and preserved in a strong acidic sauce. Most cooks keep a selection of homemade pickles on hand and serve them with rice and curries.

Fresh coconut chutney is by far the most popular chutney in Kerala. This spicy condiment is always served with *dosas* (crepes) and *idlis* (dumplings)—the South Indian snacks that are now popular in the North. Coconut chutney can be white in color, green from herbs, or pale reddish from red chilies. The consistency can vary too: it is thick when served with rice, or more liquid when eaten

A spice box brimming with black peppercorns.

with *dosa* and *idli*. Since coconut doesn't keep long, this chutney should always be made the day it is eaten.

Hot and tangy pickles are designed to add extra spark to your meal. There is usually a jar of them on the dinner table and everyone helps themselves to as little or as much as they have a taste for. Favorites in Kerala include pickled limes, unripe mangoes, green peppercorns, and mouth-puckering gooseberries. At a feast, there is a spot on the upper-right corner of the banana leaf reserved for them, and if you are looking for a palate cleanser at the end of the meal, you can nibble on your pickles.

It is surprising how easy pickles are to prepare. Gingelly (light sesame) oil is the preferred medium for frying the pickling spices (mustard seeds, fenugreek seeds, asafetida, and red chili). It is important to have very clean, dry, airtight jars for storing, and to bottle the ingredients after they have cooled completely in jars that have been rinsed with boiling water and air-dried. Pickles keep for a month in the refrigerator.

Salads are few in Kerala, possibly because some of the vegetable curries such as *pachadi* and *kichadi* are essentially lightly cooked salads. Sometimes my aunt slices up fresh vegetables and dresses them with lime juice and green chili for a simple refreshing side dish. The Muslims in Kerala have a dish called *kachumber*, similar to the North Indian yogurt salad, *raita*, which they serve with *biriyani*, but which is delicious with any meal.

White Coconut Chutney

Red Coconut Chutney

Green Coconut Chutney

Sweet Green Mango Chutney

Hot Mango Pickle

Lime Pickle

Tomato and Cucumber Salad

Yogurt Salad *(Kachumber)*

White Coconut Chutney

2 teaspoons channa dhal or yellow
   split peas
1 cup grated unsweetened coconut
1 tablespoon chopped onion
1 teaspoon chopped ginger
1 fresh green chili (serrano or Thai),
   stemmed
12 to 16 fresh curry leaves
1 teaspoon fresh lemon juice
2 tablespoons vegetable oil
$^1/_2$ teaspoon mustard seeds
1 teaspoon urad dhal (optional)
1 dried red chili

Coconut chutney is a favorite condiment for such fermented South Indian snacks as crepes (*dosa*), dumplings (*idli*), and thick pancakes (*uthappam*). My father makes this particular one with ground dhal for extra body.

1. In a blender or mini food processor, process the channa dhal until it resembles fine cornmeal.
2. Combine the ground-up channa dhal, coconut, onion, ginger, green chili, 6 to 8 of the curry leaves, lemon juice, and 1 cup of water in a blender or food processor. Scrape down the sides, and add another $^1/_4$ cup water or more as needed to form a smooth mixture the texture of thin pea soup. Set aside.
3. In a small frying pan heat the oil over medium-high heat. Add the mustard seeds and cover. When the mustard seeds have popped, put in the urad dhal and fry for a few seconds until the dhal turns pale gold. Toss in the dried red chili and the remaining curry leaves. When the curry leaves have crackled for a few seconds, add the coconut mixture to the pan, and remove from the heat; stir to combine. Cover until ready to serve.

PREPARATION TIME: 20 MINUTES
SERVES: 6 TO 8
YIELD: ABOUT 1$^1/_2$ CUPS
RECIPE MAY BE PREPARED AN HOUR IN ADVANCE THROUGH STEP 2.
   COVER BUT DO NOT REFRIGERATE; IF THE MIXTURE THICKENS
   ADD MORE WATER. COCONUT CHUTNEY SHOULD ALWAYS BE EATEN
   THE DAY IT IS MADE.

Red Coconut Chutney

6 dried red chilies

$^1/_4$ teaspoon tamarind concentrate

1 cup grated unsweetened coconut

2 tablespoons chopped shallots

1 teaspoon minced ginger

$^1/_4$ teaspoon cayenne

1 teaspoon salt

2 tablespoons vegetable oil

$^1/_2$ teaspoon mustard seeds

8 to 10 curry leaves

PREPARATION TIME: 35 MINUTES

YIELD: APPROXIMATELY 1 $^1/_2$ CUPS

SERVES: 6 TO 8

RECIPE MAY BE PREPARED AN HOUR
IN ADVANCE THROUGH STEP 3.
COVER BUT DO NOT REFRIGER-
ATE; IF MIXTURE THICKENS ADD
MORE WATER. COCONUT CHUT-
NEY SHOULD ALWAYS BE EATEN
THE DAY IT IS MADE.

This coconut chutney with red chilies is my family's favorite. It comes out looking more orange than red, and it looks pretty on a plate with Sourdough Crepes (page 40) or Sourdough Dumplings (page 46).

1. Break five of the dried red chilies in half and let the seeds fall out. Discard the seeds and place the skins in a small saucepan with 1 $^1/_4$ cups water and bring to a boil. Turn off the heat and set aside for 10 minutes.

2. In a small bowl combine the tamarind concentrate with 2 tablespoons of hot water and use your fingers to dissolve the tamarind. Set aside.

3. Drain the chilies, and reserve the liquid. Put the chilies in a blender with the coconut, shallots, ginger, cayenne, salt, and enough of the reserved chili liquid to blend thoroughly and obtain the consistency of thin pea soup. Use additional water if necessary. Set aside.

4. In a frying pan heat the oil, add the mustard seeds, and cover. When the seeds have popped, add the remaining whole dried red chili and the curry leaves. After the leaves crackle for a few seconds, pour the coconut mixture into the pan; remove from the heat and stir to combine. Taste for salt. Cover until ready to serve.

Green Coconut Chutney

1 cup grated unsweetened coconut

1 tablespoon chopped onion

1 fresh green chili (serrano or Thai), chopped

1 1/2 teaspoons chopped ginger

1/4 cup loosely packed fresh cilantro leaves

3/4 teaspoon salt

1 teaspoon fresh lime juice

1/4 cup plain yogurt

2 tablespoons vegetable oil

1/2 teaspoon mustard seeds

2 dried red chilies

8 to 10 fresh curry leaves

Fresh cilantro makes this chutney pale green, and you can make it spicier by adding more green chili. It makes a nice dipping sauce for Spiced Meat Samosas (page 62) and Dhal Fritters (page 59), or a side dish with Lamb *Biriyani* (page 170).

1. Combine the coconut, onion, green chili, ginger, cilantro, salt, lime juice, yogurt, and about 1 cup water in a blender. Blend thoroughly, using additional water as needed to get the consistency of thin pea soup. Set aside.

2. In a frying pan heat the oil over medium-high heat. Add the mustard seeds and cover. When the seeds pop, toss in the dried red chilies and curry leaves. After the leaves crackle for a few seconds pour the coconut mixture into the pan. Stir to combine and remove from the heat.

PREPARATION TIME: 20 MINUTES

SERVES: 6 TO 8

YIELD: ABOUT 1 1/2 CUPS

RECIPE MAY BE PREPARED AN HOUR IN ADVANCE THROUGH STEP 2. COVER BUT DO NOT REFRIGERATE; IF MIXTURE THICKENS ADD MORE WATER. COCONUT CHUTNEY SHOULD ALWAYS BE EATEN THE DAY IT IS MADE.

Sweet Green Mango Chutney

1 large green (unripe) mango (about 1¹/₄ pounds)

1 cup sugar

2 tablespoons minced garlic

2 tablespoons minced ginger

³/₄ teaspoon cayenne

2 tablespoons white vinegar

This is Haseena Sadick's recipe for a Mappila-style chutney to accompany Lamb or Fish *Biriyani* (pages 170 and 172). I think it also pairs well with Spicy Beef Curry (page 153) or Peppery Stir-Fried Lamb (page 156). It's very easy to make, and keeps well.

1. Peel the mango with a vegetable peeler; slice the flesh off the pit and coarsely chop it. Process in a food processor until minced but not pulverized. (If you don't have a food processor, mince by hand—a blender won't work here.) Place the mango in a bowl and mix in the sugar. Cover with plastic wrap and set aside for at least 18 hours at room temperature.

2. In a wide nonstick pan combine the mango with the garlic, ginger, cayenne, and vinegar. Heat the mixture over medium-high heat until it is very thick and turns butterscotch color (about 10 minutes). Remove from the heat and set aside to cool.

3. When the mixture is completely cool, serve and/or transfer to a clean bottle.

RESTING TIME: 18 HOURS
PREPARATION TIME: 25 MINUTES
YIELD: ABOUT 1¹/₂ CUPS
RECIPE KEEPS FOR 2 MONTHS IN THE REFRIGERATOR.

Hot Mango Pickle

2 small green mangoes, or 1 large
   green mango
1 teaspoon salt
$1/4$ teaspoon fenugreek seeds
$1/2$ cup gingelly or vegetable oil
$3/4$ teaspoon mustard seeds
2 dried red chilies
$1 1/2$ tablespoons cayenne
$1/2$ teaspoon ground asafetida

My aunty makes this pickle for *Onam*, the fall harvest feast. She prefers the small sour green mangoes because they're firmer and keep longer, but the large green type can also be used to make this. Use more cayenne if you want it hotter, or add white vinegar if you like your pickles very sour. I especially like eating this on the day it's made, when the mango is still nice and firm.

1. Cut the mango flesh (skin on) into $3/4$ x $1/8$-inch matchsticks (about 2 cups). Mix with the salt, cover, and set aside overnight (at least 12 hours) in a dark place so it doesn't continue to ripen.

2. The next day, heat the fenugreek seeds in a dry frying pan over medium heat until lightly toasted. Remove from the heat and grind in a mini food processor or mortar and pestle to a fine powder. Set aside.

3. Heat the oil in a frying pan over medium-high heat. Add the mustard seeds and cover. When the mustard seeds finish popping, put in the dried red chilies and remove from the heat. Allow the oil to cool for about 30 seconds, then add the ground fenugreek, cayenne, and asafetida, stirring for a minute off the heat. (The spices will burn if the oil is too hot.) Set aside to cool.

4. When the seasoned oil is completely cool, remove the red chilies. Add the mango pieces and combine thoroughly. Place the mixture in a clean, airtight jar, packing it down so no air pockets exist and a layer of oil covers the top (add more oil if

necessary). It can be eaten immediately, but the flavor deepens if the chutney is allowed to sit at room temperature for a couple of days.

RESTING TIME: 12 HOURS
PREPARATION TIME: 20 MINUTES
YIELD: ABOUT 1 1/2 CUPS
RECIPE KEEPS FOR 1 MONTH IN THE REFRIGERATOR.

Lime Pickle

Replace the mango with five small limes. In a saucepan bring about a quart of water to a boil. Add the whole limes and as soon as the water returns to a boil, cover, and remove from the heat. Set aside for about 5 minutes or until the skin is tender. Drain and cool completely. Cut each lime into quarters, then cut each quarter across in half, forming a triangle, not a segment. Sprinkle the pieces with 1 teaspoon salt, cover, and set aside overnight (at least 12 hours). Continue with steps 2 through 4. This pickle can be eaten after a day or two at room temperature and keeps in the refrigerator for a month.

Jackfruit, plentiful in Kerala, can grow to be the largest fruit in the world.

Tomato and Cucumber Salad

2 large ripe tomatoes, cut into thin
   wedges
1 medium cucumber, peeled and
   thinly sliced
$1/2$ medium red onion, cut into very
   thin wedges
1 fresh green chili (serrano or Thai),
   cut on the diagonal into paper-thin
   slices
$1/4$ teaspoon salt
2 tablespoons fresh lime juice

Salads are not a common element in a South Indian meal, but when served they tend to be very simple like this recipe from my aunt. She arranges the vegetables in layers and sprinkles thinly sliced chilies over the top. Serve this salad with any South Indian meal.

1. In a bowl combine the tomatoes, cucumber, red onion, and green chili. Set aside for at least 10 minutes.
2. Before serving, toss the ingredients with the salt and lime juice.

PREPARATION TIME: 20 MINUTES
SERVES: 6
RECIPE MAY BE PREPARED IN ADVANCE THROUGH STEP 1.

Yogurt Salad
(Kachumber)

$^1/_2$ teaspoon cumin seeds

2 $^1/_2$ cups yogurt

2 cups chopped seeded tomato

2 cups chopped seeded cucumber

1 cup finely chopped onion

$^1/_2$ cup chopped fresh coriander, plus
a few leaves for garnish

1 teaspoon minced fresh green chili
(serrano or Thai)

$^1/_4$ teaspoon cayenne

$^1/_2$ teaspoon salt

This is always served as an accompaniment to *biriyani* in the Kerala Muslim community, but it could just as easily go with curries and rice. It is very similar to *raita*, the popular yogurt salad of North India.

1. In a small frying pan toast the cumin seeds over medium heat until they give off their aroma and are lightly browned. Remove from the heat and grind them coarsely with a mortar and pestle.
2. In a bowl combine the ground cumin seeds with all the remaining ingredients except the cilantro leaves for the garnish. Mix thoroughly and taste for salt.
3. Garnish with cilantro leaves and serve.

PREPARATION TIME: 15 MINUTES
SERVES: 6 TO 8
RECIPE MAY BE PREPARED AN HOUR IN ADVANCE THROUGH STEP 2.

Sweets and Beverages

Indians rarely eat sweets after dinner, but teatime is another matter. Like clockwork, someone is in the kitchen every afternoon at five, brewing tea and arranging sweets on a platter. They could be serving sweetmeats, slices of cake, or bowls of creamy pudding—nothing is too sweet or too rich for this hour. And since this is a culture that expects visitors to drop by at teatime, it is important to have something sweet on hand to serve them.

Traditional Indian kitchens are not equipped with ovens, so a majority of sweets are designed to be made on the stove, such as the fudgelike *burfi*, or the thickened milk pudding called *payasam* served at *Nayar* (Hindu) celebrations. Baked cakes and cookies are the specialties of the Christians, and fried egg-rich sweets with nuts and raisins are what the Mappilas (Kerala Muslims) are known for best.

Each of the sweets in this chapter could be served as

Favorite snacks with tea are Dhal Fritters (page 59) and small bananas.

"dessert," since that concept fits best into a Western menu. And the hot beverages could be sipped after dinner. The Muslim Black Tea with Lime in this chapter is actually made expressly for eating after *biriyani* to cleanse the oils from the stomach.

Coffee is grown in Kerala, and unlike most of the rest of India, which drinks tea, it is a popular morning beverage. South Indian coffee is a delicious treat, made by brewing dark-roasted powdered coffee though a metal filter so that a strong liquid called a *decoction* drips out. The *decoction* is blended with hot foamy milk, much like café latte, and the result is rich and wonderful.

Noodle Pudding (*Semiya Payasam*)

Dhal Pudding (Brown *Payasam*)

Almond Pudding (*Badam Payasam*)

Coconut *Burfi*

Carrot *Halva*

Christmas Cake

Sweet Crepes with Coconut (*Motta Kozhalappam*)

Sweet Crepes with Bananas

Egg Layer Cake (*Chattippathiri*)

Cardamom Coffee

Spice Tea (*Masala Chai*)

Black Tea with Lime (*Sulaimani*)

Noodle Pudding
(*Semiya Payasam*)

5 teaspoons Ghee (page 218)

1 cup broken (1-inch lengths) angel
  hair pasta

4 cups whole milk

1 cup sugar

1/2 cup golden raisins

1/2 cup halved or broken raw cashews

1/4 teaspoon ground cardamom

Payasams are thick, milky puddings served at feasts and special occasions in Kerala. This one is made with fine wheat noodles, and is best served warm.

1. In a large pan heat 2 teaspoons of the ghee and fry the pasta until lightly browned. Set aside.

2. In a separate heavy pan bring the milk and 2 cups water to a boil. Add the fried pasta and continue boiling for 5 minutes. Add the sugar and simmer, stirring frequently to prevent the noodles from sticking to the bottom (20 to 25 minutes). The mixture is done when it reaches the consistency of heavy cream.

3. Fry the raisins and cashew nuts in the remaining 3 teaspoons ghee until lightly browned. Add these and the cardamom to the milk, stir, and remove from the heat. Serve warm.

PREPARATION TIME: 35 MINUTES

SERVES: 8

RECIPE MAY BE PREPARED SEVERAL HOURS IN ADVANCE AND WARMED BEFORE SERVING. IT WILL THICKEN AS IT SITS.

Flower petals ready to be tossed like confetti at a festival.

Dhal Pudding
(Brown *Payasam*)

1 cup channa dhal or yellow split peas

¹/₂ cup Coconut Slices (page 220)
(optional)

2 tablespoons Ghee (page 218)

¹/₂ cup broken or halved cashews

1 cup packed brown sugar

2 tablespoons quick-cooking tapioca

¹/₂ cup canned coconut milk

¹/₂ teaspoon ground cardamom

¹/₂ teaspoon ground ginger

¹/₂ teaspoon ground cumin

PREPARATION TIME: 1 HOUR 15
MINUTES

SERVES: 8

RECIPE MAY BE PREPARED SEVERAL
HOURS IN ADVANCE AND
WARMED BEFORE SERVING.

This is a rich flavorful *payasam* (thin pudding), thickened with dhal and coconut milk. Fried coconut slices are traditionally added and lend great flavor and texture.

1. In a large bowl wash the dhal in several changes of water; drain. In a 2- to 4-quart saucepan bring the dhal and 3 cups water to a boil. Partially cover and simmer over low heat for 35 minutes (45 minutes for yellow split peas) or until the dhal pieces break under pressure from the back of a spoon. Check to make sure it doesn't boil over. Remove from the heat and mash the dhal with a potato masher or the back of a spoon until only a few whole pieces remain. Set aside.

2. Fry the coconut slices in 1 tablespoon of the ghee until golden brown. Remove the coconut with a slotted spoon and set aside. In the same pan, fry the cashews until golden. Set aside.

3. Return the cooked dhal to medium heat. Add the remaining 1 tablespoon ghee, the brown sugar, tapioca, ¹/₄ cup of the coconut milk, and ¹/₄ cup water; bring to a boil. Reduce the heat to medium and cook 15 to 20 minutes, stirring constantly, until it's the consistency of thick pea soup.

4. Add the remaining ¹/₄ cup coconut milk, the cardamom, ginger, cumin, fried coconut slices, and nuts; bring just to a boil and remove from the heat. Serve warm.

Almond Pudding
(*Badam Payasam*)

1 (7-ounce) package almond paste
2 tablespoons butter
$1/4$ cup slivered almonds
$1/4$ cup Cream of Wheat
4 cups whole milk
2 cups half and half
$3/4$ cup sugar
$1/4$ teaspoon ground cardamom

PREPARATION TIME: 50 MINUTES
SERVES: 8
RECIPE MAY BE PREPARED SEVERAL
    HOURS IN ADVANCE AND
    WARMED PRIOR TO SERVING, IF
    DESIRED.

The traditional way of preparing this dish involves soaking, peeling, and grinding almonds. I find using store-bought almond paste makes this thick, satisfying dessert infinitely easier to prepare.

1. Break up the almond paste into small pieces and set aside.
2. In a large heavy pot or Dutch oven melt 1 tablespoon of the butter over low heat. Fry the almonds until golden; remove with a slotted spoon and set aside for garnish.
3. Add the remaining 1 tablespoon butter to the same pot and melt. Add the Cream of Wheat and stir constantly over medium-low heat until the grains are toasted to a pale brown.
4. Add the milk slowly, stirring constantly with a wire whisk. Add the half and half, sugar, and crumbled almond paste and whisk vigorously to break up all the solids. Increase the heat to medium-high and bring to a boil. Reduce the heat and simmer, stirring frequently to prevent sticking, until the mixture reduces by one third and coats a spoon, about 30 minutes.
5. Add the cardamom and mix thoroughly. Remove from the heat and when the pudding has slightly cooled transfer it to a serving bowl. Serve warm or at room temperature, garnished with the fried almonds. (The mixture will thicken as it cools.)

Coconut *Burfi*

1/2 teaspoon unsalted butter

1 1/2 cups sugar

3 cups sweetened shredded coconut

1/4 cup nonfat dry milk

1/4 cup half and half

2 tablespoons Ghee (page 218)

1/4 teaspoon almond extract

PREPARATION TIME: 30 MINUTES

YIELD: 25

RECIPE MAY BE PREPARED HOURS
    IN ADVANCE, AND IT KEEPS FOR
    UP TO A WEEK.

My father helped me develop this recipe for my favorite Indian confection. *Burfi* is a fudgelike sweet, but this one has a texture like chewy shortbread. It tastes best the day it's made.

1. Line an 8 x 8-inch square baking pan with aluminum foil. Smear the foil with the butter; set aside.

2. In a large deep nonstick pan bring the sugar and 3/4 cup water to a boil. Continue boiling over medium heat until the syrup becomes gummy and reaches the thread stage (about 20 minutes). Add the coconut, nonfat dry milk, and half and half, and stir constantly over medium heat until it thickens. Add the ghee and almond extract and keep stirring, turning the mixture over to cook evenly. A fine white foam will appear around the edges of the mass after about 10 minutes; continue stirring until no more liquid is visible and it forms a single semidry mass. Immediately turn onto the buttered foil and spread out to a 1/2-inch-thick layer (the surface will be rough). After a minute the surface should appear dry and any bits stuck to the spatula should be dry, not sticky. (If the *burfi* is still sticky, return it to the pan and continue frying until it appears drier, and repeat with clean, buttered foil.)

3. After cooling for 10 minutes, remove the foil (with the *burfi* on it) from the baking pan and place on a cutting board. With a long sharp knife cut the *burfi* into squares or diamonds. Serve when completely cool, or store it in an airtight container.

Carrot *Halva*

1/2 teaspoon unsalted butter
3/4 pound peeled carrots
3 cups whole milk
3 tablespoons Ghee (page 218)
1 cup sugar
1/3 cup golden raisins
1/3 cup sliced almonds
1/4 teaspoon ground cardamom

This sweet carrot compote, with nuts and raisins, is equally well loved in North and South India. Serve it warm so the butter doesn't solidify, and eat it with a spoon.

1. Butter a shallow 1-quart serving bowl.
2. Coarsely grate the carrots in a food processor fitted with a shredding disk, or with a box grater (about 3 cups).
3. In a deep heavy-bottomed pan or Dutch oven combine the grated carrots and milk; bring to a boil. Reduce the heat to medium and stir constantly until the mixture thickens and no more liquid appears at the bottom of the pan (about 30 minutes).
4. Add the ghee and sugar and continue stirring. As the sugar melts the mixture will appear runny again. Stir until it is no longer watery and the color has darkened (about 15 minutes).
5. Add the raisins, almonds, and cardamom and stir continuously until the mixture dries out, starts to draw away from the sides of the pan, and moves as a solid mass. Immediately remove from the heat and pour the mixture into the buttered serving bowl. It should be the consistency of stiff rice pudding. Keep it covered until serving. Serve warm, spooned into small dishes.

PREPARATION TIME: 1 1/4 HOURS
SERVES: 6 TO 8
RECIPE MAY BE PREPARED A FEW HOURS IN ADVANCE AND WARMED BEFORE SERVING.

Christmas Cake

9 tablespoons vegetable shortening

2 cups mixed candied fruits (any combination of orange peel, lemon peel, pineapple, or citron)

1 cup golden raisins

1/4 cup brandy or dark rum

5 tablespoons granulated sugar

9 tablespoons unsalted butter

2 1/2 cups confectioners' sugar, unsifted

4 large eggs, separated

1 teaspoon vanilla extract

1/2 teaspoon fresh orange zest

2 cups all-purpose flour

1/2 teaspoon ground cinnamon

1/4 teaspoon ground clove

1/8 teaspoon ground nutmeg

1/2 cup milk

This recipe was inspired by Mrs. K. M. Mathew, one of the most respected Syrian Christian cookbook authors in Kerala. It's similar to a light pound cake studded with dried fruits, spiced with cinnamon and clove, and it's made to give to friends during the holiday. As with fruitcake, this will get moister as it sits.

1. Preheat the oven to 325 degrees F. Grease two loaf pans, line them with parchment paper, and grease the paper with 1 tablespoon of vegetable shortening.

2. Chop the candied fruit into small pieces. In a saucepan combine the chopped fruit, raisins, and brandy and heat over very low heat for 10 minutes to steam the fruit. Set aside.

3. In a heavy pan melt 3 tablespoons of the sugar over medium heat. When it turns caramel color, add 1/2 cup boiling water, stirring to avoid lumps. Continue heating without stirring until it appears to be dark, syrupy, and very bubbly (the thread stage). Remove the pan from the heat and place it in a larger pan of simmering water to keep the caramel from hardening.

4. Cream the butter and 8 tablespoons of vegetable shortening until light and fluffy. Slowly add the confectioners' sugar and cream well.

5. Add the egg yolks to the creamed mixture one at a time, mixing well between each one. Stir in the vanilla and orange zest.

6. In another bowl combine the flour, cinnamon, clove, and nutmeg. Alternately add the flour and milk to the creamed

mixture. When the batter is well mixed, add the steamed fruits and hot caramel. Mix thoroughly.

7. In a separate bowl, whip the egg whites and the remaining 2 tablespoons sugar to form stiff peaks. Fold into the batter. Pour the batter into the prepared loaf pans and bake for 1 hour until the tops are nicely browned and a cake tester comes out clean.

8. When cool, remove the parchment paper from the loaves, wrap them well, and store in an airtight container. This cake keeps for 2 weeks.

PREPARATION TIME: 1 HOUR
BAKING TIME: 1 HOUR
YIELD: 2 LOAVES
RECIPE SHOULD BE PREPARED AT LEAST 1 DAY IN ADVANCE.

Sweet Crepes with Coconut
(*Motta Kozhalappam*)

1 cup all-purpose flour

$^1/_4$ teaspoon baking powder

2 tablespoons sugar

$^3/_4$ cup milk

1 large egg, lightly beaten

1 tablespoon butter, melted

1 cup sweetened shredded coconut

$^1/_4$ teaspoon ground cardamom

PREPARATION TIME: 40 MINUTES

SERVES: 6

YIELD: 12 TO 14

RECIPE MAY BE PREPARED AN HOUR
IN ADVANCE THROUGH STEP 2.
BATTER SHOULD BE STORED IN
THE REFRIGERATOR.

These are light pancakes wrapped around a sweet coconut filling. Nimmy Paul recommends baking them at the end to make the edges crispy instead of soft, but that step is optional.

1. In a bowl combine the dry ingredients. Add the milk, egg, melted butter, and $^3/_4$ cup water. Whisk until combined and no lumps remain. The mixture should coat a spoon and have the consistency of thin pancake batter.

2. Combine the coconut and cardamom in a bowl; set aside.

3. Heat an 8-inch nonstick frying pan over medium heat. When the pan is hot, stir the batter and ladle a scant $^1/_4$ cup onto the pan. Immediately lift the pan and tilt it in a circular direction to spread the batter into a thin even circle like a crepe. If it doesn't spread easily, add a little more water to the batter in the bowl. Cook until the underside is lightly browned. Do not flip. Remove the pancake to a clean surface, place 1 tablespoon of the coconut mixture down the center of circle. Roll it into a cylinder and place it in a small baking dish, or alternately place it directly onto a serving platter and skip the next step.

4. If baking, preheat the oven to 325 degrees F and continue to fry the remaining pancakes, adding them to the baking dish after rolling them up. Cover the baking dish with foil and bake for 10 minutes. Remove and serve warm.

Sweet Crepes with Bananas

Buttery sautéed bananas make a nice filling for crepes. For a large dinner party, serve both versions.

Follow the directions for Sweet Crepes with Coconut (page 208) except replace the coconut and cardamom with 3 large yellow bananas (no brown spots), 2 tablespoons ghee, and 1 tablespoon sugar. Peel the bananas and cut them into $1/2$-inch rounds. Melt the ghee in a wok over medium heat. Add the banana slices and sauté until the bananas begin to soften. Sprinkle with the sugar and stir until the mixture becomes soft and sticky but the bananas still hold their shape. Fill each crepe with a scant $1/4$ cup of banana. Serve warm.

PREPARATION TIME: 40 MINUTES
SERVES: 6
YIELD: 12 TO 14

Egg Layer Cake
(*Chattippathiri*)

6 flour tortillas, preferably 6 inches in
   diameter
2 1/2 teaspoons Ghee plus
   5 tablespoons melted Ghee
   (page 218)
1/2 cup raw cashews, coarsely
   chopped
1/2 cup golden raisins
4 extra-large eggs
1/2 cup plus 1 teaspoon sugar
1/2 teaspoon ground cardamom
1/2 cup whole milk

PREPARATION TIME: 1 HOUR
BAKING TIME: 50 TO 55 MINUTES
SERVES: 6 TO 8
RECIPE MAY BE PREPARED A FEW
   HOURS IN ADVANCE AND COOLED
   COMPLETELY BEFORE SERVING.

This is a Mappila sweet that has alternating layers of flat bread and egg filling, and a pleasant kugel-like texture. I use tortillas as a shortcut rather than making flatbread from scratch.

1. If the tortillas are larger than 6 inches, stack them up and cut them down to a 6-inch diameter.
2. Heat 2 teaspoons of the ghee in a frying pan. Sauté the cashews until browned. Remove the cashews and set aside. Fry the raisins in the ghee remaining in the pan until puffy and light brown. Set aside.
3. In a bowl beat the eggs, 1/2 cup of the sugar, and the cardamom.
4. Pour the milk into a seperate bowl.
5. Rub 1/2 teaspoon ghee in a 6-inch soufflé dish or other ovenproof pan that just fits the tortillas. Heat the oven to 325 degrees F.
6. Take one of the tortillas, dip it in the milk, then into the egg mixture, then place in the pan. Pour 3 tablespoons of egg mixture over it, sprinkle with a few cashews and raisins and 1 1/2 teaspoons melted ghee. Repeat with the other tortillas. When the last tortilla is added, sprinkle the remaining cashews, raisins, melted ghee, and 1 teaspoon sugar over the top. (Discard the leftover milk.) Cover loosely with foil and bake for 50 to 55 minutes until golden brown. Test by lifting the top tortilla and checking that the egg mixture underneath is not runny. Remove from the oven, cool, and cut into wedges. Serve with the golden side up.

Cardamom Coffee

2 cardamom pods
3 tablespoons finely ground espresso
   or other dark-roasted coffee beans
1 ¹/₂ cups whole milk
4 to 6 teaspoons sugar (according to
   taste)

I was served a tumbler of this fragrant hot coffee at a roadside restaurant in the Cardamom Hills of eastern Kerala where cardamom and coffee are both grown. I love South Indian coffee: a small amount of concentrated coffee diluted with rich foamy water-buffalo milk with lots of sugar stirred in, and this version has the added aroma of cardamom. An espresso maker or machine works well for brewing the intense coffee portion of this drink.

1. Break open the cardamom pods; remove the seeds with the tip of a knife and discard the husks. Crush the seeds in a mortar with a pestle. Place the crushed cardamom seeds and ground coffee in the basket of an espresso maker. Using ²/₃ cup water, brew the espresso according to manufacturer's directions.
2. Heat the milk and sugar together in a saucepan over medium-low heat. Whisk vigorously to foam the milk. When the milk is hot but not boiling, remove from the heat. Pour the brewed coffee into the hot milk; serve in two mugs.

PREPARATION TIME: 10 MINUTES
SERVES: 2

Spice Tea
(*Masala Chai*)

1 (2-inch) stick cinnamon

4 black peppercorns

5 whole cloves

2 cardamom pods

²/₃ cup whole milk

5 rounded teaspoons Indian black tea or Darjeeling

3 tablespoons sugar, or to taste

Indian black teas such as Taj Mahal and Red Label brands have a granular texture and strong unperfumed flavor, and I recommend using them for this warming beverage. The Indian method of brewing tea is to steep the leaves in a mixture of hot milk, water, and crushed spices. Once it's steeped, the tea is strained into a warmed teapot and served with such snacks as Sweet Dumplings (page 58), Spiced Meat Samosas (page 62), and Batter-Fried Bananas (page 61).

1. With a mortar and pestle, crush the cinnamon, peppercorns, cloves, and cardamom pods.

2. In a saucepan combine the crushed spices with milk and 4 cups water. Bring to a boil, turn off the heat, and cover for 5 minutes.

3. Add the tea and sugar, cover, and steep 3 minutes. Stir and strain into a warmed teapot or directly into teacups.

PREPARATION TIME: 10 MINUTES

SERVES: 4 TO 6

Black Tea with Lime
(*Sulaimani*)

3 teaspoons Indian black tea

3 tablespoons sugar (according to taste)

1 tablespoon fresh lime juice

Haseena Sadick from Kochi made this tea for me after serving a huge lunch that included her extraordinary Fish *Biriyani*. She says Muslims drink this after *biriyani* because they feel it cleanses the oil from the stomach. I could drink it anytime.

1. Place the tea in a teapot. Add 4 cups boiling water and steep covered for 3 minutes.

2. Add the sugar and lime juice to the teapot and stir. Serve immediately.

PREPARATION TIME: 10 MINUTES

SERVES: 4 TO 6

Essential Recipes

Ghee
Pappadam
Coconut Slices
Sambar Powder
Garam Masala

Pappadam *is dry-roasted in North India, deep-fried in the South.*

Ghee

1/2 pound (1 stick) unsalted butter

This form of clarified butter has a nutty taste and a long shelf life. It is used as a frying medium throughout India and has a richer flavor than oil. In the south it is as indispensable a companion to rice and dhal as butter is to bread. I avoid store-bought ghee because making it is simple and tastier. Ghee will keep for months, and is great to have on hand as a substitute for oil or butter in non-Indian cooking too. Try using it for sautéing vegetables or smearing on warm bread.

1. In a heavy, preferably light-colored skillet melt the butter over medium-low heat. The melted butter will sputter gently as the moisture boils out of it, and the bubbles will change from large to fine and foamy.

2. Once the foam appears, push it aside every few seconds to see if the milk solids have settled to the bottom of the pan. When this sediment appears golden brown, remove it from the heat. Do not let it turn dark brown.

3. Cool the ghee for a minute or two, then pour the liquid into a container with a tight-fitting lid, leaving most of the solids behind. Cool it completely, cover, and store at room temperature for 1 month or in the refrigerator for 3 months.

4. Ghee turns to a solid as it cools, so bring it to room temperature before using, or melt it by placing the jar in which it is stored in hot water.

PREPARATION TIME: 15 MINUTES
YIELD: ABOUT 1/2 CUP

Pappadam

Vegetable oil for deep-frying
12 plain *pappadam* (approximately
6 inches in diameter)

In North India these legume wafers are called *papad* and dry-roasted over a flame, but in the South they are deep-fried until they form lots of air bubbles and become light and puffy. They are sold in many flavors, but plain is preferred in Kerala. *Pappadam* are always part of a South Indian rice meal: they are crushed and mixed together with rice, dhal, and a little ghee, for added texture. Store-bought wafers are used almost exclusively by Indian cooks because they are labor-intensive to make and require days of drying in the hot sun.

1. Heat the oil in a large wok (*pappadam* will expand) over medium-high heat until it reaches 350 degrees F, or until a tiny piece of *pappadam* dropped in the oil quickly bobs to the top.
2. Drop one *pappadam* into the oil and let it expand to its full size (this takes only a couple of seconds). Using tongs, flip it over quickly to lightly brown the other side. Remove to a paper towel and repeat with the remaining wafers. If the *pappadam* don't become crisp immediately, the oil is too cool; if they brown too quickly, the heat is too high.
3. Serve immediately, or store in an airtight container for a few days.

PREPARATION TIME: 15 MINUTES
SERVES: 6

Coconut Slices

1 fresh coconut

A fresh coconut is required to make these tasty slices. They add a nice crunchy bite of coconut to curries and puddings. When selecting a coconut, look for one that feels heavy, has a lot of liquid inside when shaken, and is mold-free around the "eyes."

1. Preheat the oven to 375 degrees F.
2. Puncture an eye of the coconut (one of them will be soft) with an ice pick or other sharp instrument, and drain out all the coconut water. Be sure the water tastes sweet and not sour, which indicates that the coconut has spoiled. Discard the water.
3. Place the coconut on a pie pan and bake for 25 minutes. Several cracks should appear in the shell. Remove it from the oven, and using a hammer, strike the shell a few times to create more cracks. When the coconut has cooled enough to handle, pry the shell away from the meat.
4. With a vegetable peeler, remove the brown skin from the meat. Cut the meat into pieces that are $1/8$ inch thick and about $1/2$ inch wide. Freeze the unused portion.

BAKING TIME: 25 MINUTES
PREPARATION TIME: 10 MINUTES
YIELD: ABOUT 2 CUPS

Kathakali Dancer.

Sambar Powder

8 teaspoons ground coriander

2 teaspoons ground cumin

$^1/_2$ teaspoon cayenne

$^1/_2$ teaspoon turmeric

$^1/_2$ teaspoon ground black pepper

$^1/_2$ teaspoon ground asafetida

This powder is sold commercially, but it is simple to make from ingredients in your cupboard.

Blend all the ingredients together and store in an airtight jar out of the light. It will keep for 6 months.

YIELD: $^1/_4$ CUP

Garam Masala

4 whole pieces star anise
2 teaspoons fennel seeds
2 teaspoons ground cinnamon
2 teaspoons ground clove
2 teaspoons ground cardamom
1 teaspoon ground nutmeg

This recipe comes from the Muslim community in Kerala, and is a variation on the spice mix by the same name used in North India. I do not advise substituting store-bought garam masala in the recipes in this book because it will change the flavor of the dishes.

1. Place the star anise in a coffee grinder and grind to a fine powder. Measure out 2 teaspoonfuls, reserving the rest for another use.
2. Grind the fennel seeds in the coffee grinder to form a fine powder.
3. Combine all the ingredients and store in an airtight jar away from the light. It will keep for 6 months.

YIELD: 1/4 CUP

Old-fashioned flair at the Indian Coffee House in Kottayam.

Bibliography

Abdulla, Ummi. *Malabar Muslim Cookery*. Bombay: Orient Longman, 1981.

Achaya, K. T. *Indian Food, A Historical Companion*. Oxford, England: Oxford University Press, 1994.

Bharadwaj, Monisha. *The Indian Pantry*. London: Thomas Goode, 1996.

Chaitanya, Krishna. *Kerala*. New Delhi: National Book Trust, India, 1994.

Chakravarty, Indira. *Saga of Indian Food*. New Delhi: Sterling Publishers, 1972.

Franke, Richard, and Barbara Chasin. "Development Without Growth: The Kerala Experiment." *Technology Review*, April 1990, 42–51.

Fuller, C. J. *The Nayars Today*. Cambridge, England: Cambridge University Press, 1976.

Herbst, Sharon Tyler. *The New Food Lover's Companion, Second Edition*. Happauge, N.Y.: Barron's Educational Series, 1995.

Hyman, Mavis. *Indian-Jewish Cooking*. London: Hyman Publishers, 1993.

Jaffrey, Madhur. *A Taste of India*. New York: Atheneum, 1988.

Koder, S. S. *History of the Jews of Kerala*. Cochin, Kerala, India, 1974.

Koya, S. M. Mohamed. *Mappilas of Malabar: Studies in Social and Cultural History*. Calicut, India: Sandhya Publications, 1983.

Mathew, K. M. *The Family Cookbook*. Kottayam, India: National Book Stall, 1987.

————. *Kerala Cookery*. Kottayam, India: National Book Stall, 1986.

Mayer, Adrian C. *Land and Society in Malabar*. London: Oxford University Press, 1952.

Menon, A. Sreedhara. *Cultural Heritage of Kerala*. Madras, India: S. Viswanathan Private Limited, 1996.

Miller, Roland E. *Mappila Muslims of Kerala: A Study in Islamic Trends*. Madras, India: Orient Longman, 1976.

Norman, Jill. *The Complete Book of Spices: A Practical Guide to Spices and Aromatic Seeds*. New York: Penguin Books, 1995.

Panikkar, T. K. Gopal. *Malabar and Its Folk*. New Delhi: Asian Educational Services, 1983.

Patil, Vimla. *A Cook's Tour of South India*. New Delhi: Sterling Publishers Private Limited, 1998.

Roden, Claudia. *The Book of Jewish Food: An Odyssey from Samarkand to New York*. New York: Alfred A. Knopf, 1996.

Sahni, Julie. *Classic Indian Cooking*. New York: William Morrow, 1980.

Solomon, Charmaine. *Encyclopedia of Asian Food*. Boston: Periplus Editions (HK), 1998.

Varughese, B. F. *Herbivore: Exclusive Vegetarian Cuisine*. Kottayam, India: Bailey Press.

Vijay, G. Padma. *101 Kerala Delicacies*. Calcutta, India: Rupa, 1998.

Woodcock, George. *Kerala: A Portrait of the Malabar Coast*. London: Faber and Faber, 1967.

Index